# NORSE PAGANISM FOR BEGINNERS

*EXPLORE THE HISTORY OF THE OLD NORSE RELIGION- ÁSATRÚ, COSMOLOGY, MYTHOLOGY, MAGIC, RUNES, TAROT, WITCHCRAFT, & MORE*

HISTORY BROUGHT ALIVE

© **Copyright 2022 - All rights reserved.**

The content contained within this book may not be reproduced, duplicated, or transmitted without direct written permission from the author or the publisher.

Under no circumstances will any blame or legal responsibility be held against the publisher, or author, for any damages, reparation, or monetary loss due to the information contained within this book, either directly or indirectly.

Legal Notice:

This book is copyright protected. It is only for personal use. You cannot amend, distribute, sell, use, quote, or paraphrase any part, or the content within this book, without the consent of the author or publisher.

Disclaimer Notice:

Please note the information contained within this document is for educational and entertainment purposes only. All effort has been executed to present accurate, up-to-date, reliable, complete information. No warranties of any kind are declared or implied. Readers acknowledge that the author is not engaged in the rendering of legal, financial, medical, or professional advice. The content within this book has been derived from various sources. Please consult a licensed professional before attempting any techniques outlined in this book.

By reading this document, the reader agrees that under no circumstances is the author responsible for any losses, direct or indirect, that are incurred as a result of the use of the information contained within this document, including, but not limited to, errors, omissions, or inaccuracies.

# FREE BONUS FROM HBA: EBOOK BUNDLE

Greetings!

First of all, thank you for reading our books. As fellow passionate readers of History and Mythology, we aim to create the very best books for our readers.

Now, we invite you to join our VIP list. As a welcome gift, we offer the History & Mythology Ebook Bundle below for free. Plus you can be the first to receive new books and exclusives! <u>Remember it's 100% free to join.</u>

Simply scan the QR code to join.

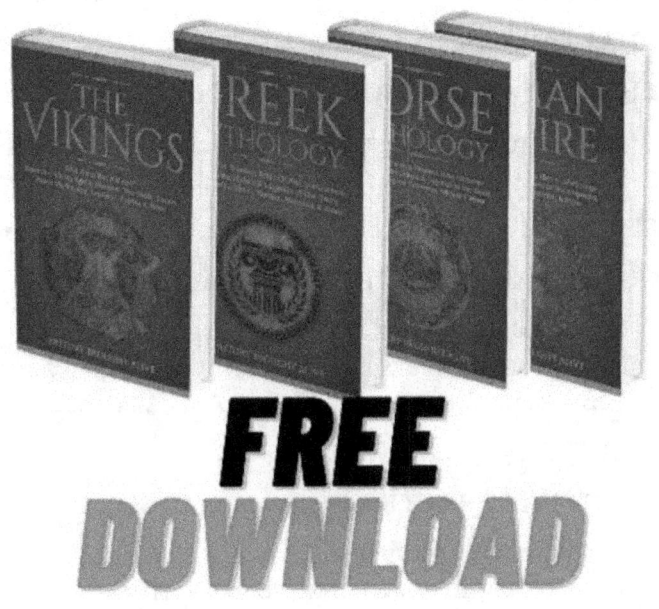

**Keep up to date with us on:**
YouTube: History Brought Alive
Facebook: History Brought Alive
www.historybroughtalive.com

# CONTENTS

**INTRODUCTION** ............................................. 1
   THE SOLUTION ............................................ 4

**CHAPTER 1** ..................................................... 9
**THE HISTORY OF NORSE PAGANISM** ............ 9
   WHO PRACTICED NORSE PAGANISM? .......................... 11
   IN SUMMARY ............................................... 25

**CHAPTER 2** ................................................... 26
**NORSE PAGAN BELIEFS AND VALUES** ......... 26
   NORSE PAGAN BELIEFS ..................................... 27
   NORSE PAGAN VALUES ..................................... 33
   IN SUMMARY ............................................... 38

**CHAPTER 3** ................................................... 39
**SPIRITUAL PRACTICES** ............................... 39
   THE WAY OF FIRE AND ICE ................................ 41
   THE TYPES OF RITUALS INVOLVED IN SPIRITUAL PRACTICES ............................................... 43
   NORSE PAGAN SACRED SPACES ........................... 51
   NORSE PAGAN FESTIVALS THAT ARE STILL CELEBRATED TODAY .................................................... 55

**CHAPTER 4** ................................................... 63
**THE POETTIC EDDA AND THE PROSE EDDA** . 63
   THE EDDAS ............................................... 64
   THE SAGAS ............................................... 70
   THE LITERARY TEXTS IN THE MODERN WORLD ............ 73
   IN SUMMARY ............................................... 74

**CHAPTER 5** ................................................... 76

## THE NORSE PAGAN CREATION MYTH .......... 76

COSMOLOGY .................................................................. 77
THE CREATION OF THE WORLD ................................. 79
WHY UNDERSTANDING THE CREATION MYTH IS
IMPORTANT ................................................................. 85

## CHAPTER 6 ........................................................ 87

## THE NINE REALMS ........................................... 87

AN INTRODUCTION TO EACH OF THE NINE REALMS ...... 88
WHY IS IT IMPORTANT TO UNDERSTAND THE NINE
REALMS? ..................................................................... 95

## CHAPTER 7 ....................................................... 96

## MYTHOLOGICAL GODS, CREATURES, AND BEINGS ............................................................... 96

THE NORSE PAGAN GODS AND GODDESSES .................. 97
CREATURES AND BEINGS ............................................ 109
THE IMPORTANCE OF UNDERSTANDING THE GODS,
CREATURES, AND BEINGS IN NORSE MYTHOLOGY ....... 127

## CHAPTER 8 ..................................................... 129

## RAGNARÖK ..................................................... 129

THE END OF DAYS ...................................................... 130
THE IMPORTANCE OF UNDERSTANDING RAGNARÖK .... 134

## CHAPTER 9 ..................................................... 135

## MAGIC IN NORSE PAGANISM ....................... 135

NORSE PAGAN MAGIC AND SHAMANISM ..................... 136
THE TYPES OF NORSE PAGAN MAGIC .......................... 138
THE IMPORTANCE OF UNDERSTANDING THE DIFFERENT
TYPES OF NORSE PAGAN MAGIC PATHS ...................... 146

## CHAPTER 10 .................................................... 148

## RUNES, TAROT AND ASTROLOGY ............... 148
- Runes ................................................................ 149
- Tarot .................................................................161
- Astrology ........................................................ 164

## CHAPTER 11 ................................................... 170

## NORSE PAGAN PATHWAYS ......................... 170
- The Different Pathways ............................... 171

## CHAPTER 12 ................................................... 189

## NORSE PAGANISM IN THE MODERN WORLD ............................................................................ 189
- Norse Pagan Misconceptions ............................... 191
- The Revival of Norse Paganism ........................... 195

## CONCLUSION ................................................. 199
- What did we cover? ............................................. 200
- Did We Deliver Our Promise? ............................. 213
- What Will You Take Away From This Book? ....... 214

## REFERENCES .................................................. 215

## OTHER BOOKS BY HISTORY BROUGHT ALIVE ............................................................................ 227

## FREE BONUS BOOK FROM HBA: EBOOK BUNDLE ........................................................... 230

# INTRODUCTION

Norse Paganism is known by many names, such as "Norse Mythology" and "Old Norse Religion". When you read the name "Norse Mythology", you probably imagine the muscular, blonde, hammer-wielding superhero whose face has become synonymous with the name Thor, the god of thunder. While Norse Paganism certainly has its own Thor, he is nothing like his movie counterpart.

In reality, Norse Paganism is quite different from its more well-known media counterparts. Popular series about Vikings and their battles against Rome and the Christians are based on the true stories and mythology of the Norse people, but the keyword here is 'based'. The creators of these works used the true story as inspiration to create a new, albeit misinformed, version of who the Norse people were and what they believed in.

True, the Norse people did have fierce warriors who fought in battles and sailed long distances in longboats to find new lands, but the Norse Pagans were mainly an agricultural community. Even when they traveled to places such as the British Isles and Iceland, they adapted to the culture and belief systems of the area in which they decided to settle. This sliver of truth, however, is counteracted by the misinformation created through the artistic license taken by movie directors.

There is no scholarly basis for the Norse Pagans depicted in the media. The beliefs and mythology of the Norse Pagans have been twisted to benefit those who are seeking symbols of power. A hammer-wielding, muscular god definitely supports an image of power. However, this means that the image and tone of the Norse Pagans in the media usually has a political, and even racist undertone, that negatively impacts the truth behind their beliefs and practices.

This twisting of the Norse Pagan image to benefit those seeking an image of power has affected the credibility of the information on the Vikings and Norse Pagans on the internet. You need to refer to multiple sources, after verifying their credibility, to answer a single question, which can be quite discouraging when you want to learn more about the Norse Pagans and their beliefs.

## The Solution

Norse Paganism is a polytheistic, oral culture that developed from pre-Christian, Germanic religion. The polytheistic nature of Norse Paganism means that those who embrace this belief system worshiped more than one god and/or goddess. They obtained their knowledge about the belief system from stories told by their elders, who received this knowledge from their previous generations. As such, very few written texts exist from before the introduction of Christianity to Northern Europe.

The arrival of Christians in Northern Europe allowed for the interaction of the two opposing belief systems. Each side would draw parallels between their belief system and the other's system, in order to better understand these new beliefs. This interaction has been reflected in the written records of Norse Paganism that were created after the arrival of the Christian people. This creates the problem that there are a variety of sources detailing Norse Paganism, but certain sources have a more Christian influence; making it difficult to determine the truth behind the history of Norse Paganism without running into potential bias.

That is where *Norse Paganism for Beginners* comes in. History Brought Alive aims to provide you with a single credible source detailing Norse Paganism, its history, belief system, and who practiced these beliefs, as well as what Norse Paganism looks like in our modern world. This book has been written using a variety of scholarly articles, books written by scholars of Norse Paganism, as well as books that contain the translations of the few existing original texts of the Norse people.

The knowledge provided by this book is non-partisan. The descriptions and explanations will be detailed, but easy to understand, so that you can learn from them without feeling overwhelmed.

History Brought Alive aims to provide readers with an informative and entertaining source of information that details the history behind the mythology, culture, and belief systems of the people who came before us. They pride themselves on the accuracy and credibility of the information contained in their books. One of their books that can be read in addition to *Norse Paganism for Beginners* includes *Norse Mythology, Vikings, Magic & Runes*. The focus of this book is on the Viking people and their folklore, as well as the magic of runes.

### **The Benefits of Reading this Book**
While this book cannot provide you with the

intricate knowledge of every single aspect of Norse Paganism, it will provide you with more than a bare-bones knowledge of what Norse Paganism is without overwhelming you. You will walk away from this book with an understanding of the truth behind Norse Paganism and its history, people, and practices. Your knowledge will be accurate and detailed, allowing you to educate your family members the next time you watch a series that inaccurately depicts who the Norse Pagans were.

## Our Promise to You

History Brought Alive aims to provide its readers with new insight into the cultures, religions, and mythology of both present and past societies, in a format that is more than the basics provided by other books. You will gain knowledge from a single, accurate source that uses the hard-won knowledge of scholars in a non-partisan manner, while being entertaining.

We aim to make learning fun without the overwhelming feeling of having to do the research yourself.

Don't waste another minute, everything you need to know is one page away. So get comfortable, turn the page, and get ready to be transported into a world of myth, magic, and adventure: the world of Norse Paganism.

# CHAPTER 1
# THE HISTORY OF NORSE PAGANISM

Norse Paganism is a North Germanic religion that was passed down orally, from the elders in the community to their children. This polytheistic religion focuses on ritual practices which Norse people integrated into their everyday life. Essentially, Norse Paganism was not just a religion, but a way of living. It is based on the practices and beliefs of pre-Christian Scandinavia. The origins of this religion date back to the Scandinavian Iron Age (500-400

BCE), however, its expressions have been traced back as far as the Bronze Age (1700-500 BCE) and are possibly neolithic in origin.

To understand what Norse Paganism is, it is important to understand what the two words mean by themselves:

- **Norse:** the word 'Norse' relates to the group of Germanic languages and the inhabitants of ancient Scandinavia.
- **Pagan:** paganism is not necessarily a set religion, instead, it refers to an unconverted person whose beliefs are neither Christianity, Judaism, nor Islam.
- **Polytheistic:** this means that the Norse Pagans worshiped and/or believed in multiple deities, or, as they called them, gods and goddesses.

Therefore; it is reasonable to say that Norse

Paganism is the belief system of a person who lived in ancient Scandinavia, or spoke one of the Germanic languages, and followed a set of beliefs that they integrated into their daily life. These beliefs were neither Christian, Judaic, or Islamic in origin.

Norse Paganism has many names. The names that are more commonly known include 'Norse Mythology' and 'Old Norse Religion'. These names are used interchangeably with slight variations, but they all refer to Norse Paganism.

## Who Practiced Norse Paganism?

To understand what Norse Paganism is and where it comes from, it is important to have a basic understanding of the people who followed this belief system. The Germanic tribes who followed the beliefs of Norse Paganism were originally agricultural communities, as evidenced by the fact that the chieftain or leader of the community would have the largest farm. Their soil would be the most fertile, and they would have large herds of cattle and sheep to graze. The chief would lead multiple farmsteads and would compete to gain the favor of farmers by consuming their harvests, giving them gifts, and participating in legal contests. Chieftains would also share their wealth with those in their community, host feasts, and play an important role in spiritual practices and celebrations. The spiritual practices of these tribes were largely based on a sense of community and the farming seasons.

Norse Paganism is described as a North Germanic religion. The word 'Germanic' is used to describe the people who originally spoke the same language in pre-Christian Scandinavia. These people shared a common tongue that was split when those who spoke the language broke off to form new tribes. The language and culture of these new tribes evolved as they adapted to live in different regions.

These new linguistic branches consisted of the North Germanic branch, which included the Norse and Scandinavian dialects; the East Germanic branch, consisting of the Gothic language; and the West Germanic branch. This branch consists of English and the continental high and low German dialects that we are familiar with today.

The variation in linguistic branches fits the fact that Norse Paganism is an oral culture. Norse Pagan beliefs and spiritual practices were passed on from the tribe's elders to the younger generation through verbal retellings and stories of their gods and spiritual practices. This resulted in very few written accounts of Norse Paganism existing before the Christianisation of Northern Europe.

The written sources used to piece together this religion vary wildly in their origin, with everything from primary sources like the *Prose Edda,* post-Christian Old Norse manuscripts like the *Hávamál,* Roman sources, and archeological evidence like runic inscriptions. Tacitus and Julius Caesar compiled the Roman sources on the Norse Pagan people. However, the archeological evidence was the most widespread, with runic inscriptions found everywhere from tools, to jewelry, to weapons. The information contained in these sources was used by scholars to better understand Norse Paganism and the people who followed this belief system.

The beliefs of the new tribes were called Germanic Mythology. This term encompasses the organized expression of the Northern European people and their beliefs, otherwise known as Paganism by the Christians. While their religion was called pagan, in reality, it was merely their version of how they led their lives. As agricultural people, they shared a common background that provided a foundation and common origin for Norse Paganism. The introduction of foreign elements occurred so that the different tribes could better adapt to their environment and improve their way of life. This created slight differences in how Norse Paganism was practiced and passed on by these communities.

## *The Historical Development of the Norse Pagan Community*

The historical developments of the Norse Pagan community are brief, as a result of poor documentation from before the arrival of the Christians. This issue arose due to the oral nature of Norse Pagan culture. Its beliefs, practices, and other details were passed on verbally to the younger generations, who adapted these practices to better suit their lives. Some textual descriptions of Norse Paganism do exist; however, the majority are written after the introduction of Christianity. This creates the possibility that certain details are inaccurate as a result of the Christian influence on Norse society.

This is understandable, as the writers of the time would attempt to interpret any Norse writings and belief systems by drawing parallels to their own belief systems. Using the knowledge that you have to understand something unknown is not a new concept, but it does create the issue that certain texts were influenced, tainting their accuracy. Even though not much is known of the exact origins of Norse Paganism, it is important to look at the information that is available to understand how Norse Paganism has changed as those who followed this belief system adapted to the world.

## The Iron Age (500-400 BCE)

Norse Paganism in the Iron Age began to change as the Germanic people began branching off into different directions, creating new tribes with a slightly different language, culture, and set of beliefs. This created what is called "religious parallels" between Norse Paganism and beliefs in other Germanic Societies. Essentially, there were many similarities between the type of Norse Paganism practiced by each tribe or community, however, slight variations occurred depending on where they lived, their environment, and the people that they interacted and traded with. This branching also influenced the development of the languages that they spoke.

The languages that began to form at this time were similar to the languages that we now speak in present-day Northern Germany and Denmark. Iron Age Paganism was linked to Nordic Bronze Age Paganism through certain motifs, such as the wheel cross that demonstrated a sun-orientated belief system. While this belief system died out in 500 BCE, these motifs reappeared in the late Iron Age, creating a parallel between the belief systems of this time.

## Viking Age Expansion (800-1050 AD)

When you think of Vikings, you probably think of longboats filled with warriors wearing horned helmets, carrying heavy weapons. While this image is not historically accurate, it is truthful in the fact that the Norse people during the Viking Age began to leave Scandinavia, migrating over the land or by ship, to settle further north or in other parts of Europe. A few of the known areas in which they settled include Iceland, the Faroe Islands, South-West Wales, the Western Isles, and Ireland, as well as in parts of England. Scholars called the Norse people who migrated 'settlers'.

Norse settlers brought not only their families and farming techniques, but also their belief systems. In areas such as Iceland, which did not have a monarchy, the Norse people faced little issue in introducing their beliefs to the people who resided there. Scholars believe that Thor was the more popular god of Iceland, however, the god Freyr was documented in some written sagas as having his own followers. At this time, Christians were also introducing their own beliefs to the people of Northern Europe. There is evidence suggesting that both Norse Pagan and Christian communities existed from the time the first Norse settlers arrived in Iceland.

## Christianisation (8th-12th Century)

The Norse people were introduced to Christianity through trade and travel, such as when they settled in the British Isles. The cold, harsh climate of Northern Europe discouraged people from settling there, and while that did not stop settlers from moving to these areas, it did delay their migration. This is one of the reasons why Christianity was new to areas such as Scandinavia, even though it was the widely accepted religion in most of Europe. The introduction of Christianity to these areas resulted in the conversion of some Norse Pagans to Christianity.

Not much is known about the process that was followed to convert one from Norse Paganism to Christianity, but scholars think the conversion started only a few decades after Scandinavians had migrated across Europe. It is documented, however, that Christian missionaries began to travel to Northern Europe from the British Isles at this time.

Not all areas of Northern Europe had royalty, but those that did began to convert to

Christianity. The main reasons behind the conversion of royals from Norse Paganism to Christianity were to gain military allies, as well as secure funds and political alliances. The conversion of royals meant that their people also began to partake in mass conversions. It is important to note that these mass conversions indicate that converting had more to do with one's social ties than the person believing in the Christian deities.

The royals at this time, such as King Hákon the Good, attempted to promote Christianity and convince their people to convert to it. Some of the Norse Pagans during this period fought against the idea of converting. Under King Hákon, this disagreement resulted in the burning of three churches by the Norse Pagans.

Other royals—such as king Haakon Sigurdson—only converted after being pressured into it by royals from neighboring countries. However, they still encouraged the practice of Norse Paganism. This was a common occurrence, where some Norse Pagans converted to Christianity in name, but continued to follow the practices of Norse Paganism.

Norse Pagans were not all violent about the introduction of Christianity. The polytheistic nature of Norse Paganism meant that they were quite happy to worship more than one god. To them, Christianity and Norse Paganism could co-exist because they would be adding another god to the ones that they already worship. Christian missionaries were unhappy with this idea and attempted to convince these Norse Pagans that their religions were mutually exclusive. They would have to choose between their belief systems.

The idea of introducing Christian gods into

Norse Paganism resulted in new expressions of the Pagan culture. This expression influenced myths, and resulted in retellings and written texts that had a more Christian influence. It allowed the Norse people to create a new version of Norse Paganism, one that synchronized with Christianity in a way that suited their new form of daily life.

## Post-Christian Survival (Twelfth Century to the Modern Day)

Christianity was the common, established religion of North-West Europe by the 12th century. Preachers began to condemn Norse Paganism and its followers. Norse Paganism started to become known as Old Norse mythology, as those who followed this belief system either converted to Christianity, or died of old age. It was recorded in the thirteenth century that Norse Paganism survived as an oral culture for two centuries. Old Norse mythology is still widely recognized by people in present day society, even though there are many inaccuracies displayed in books and media.

Scholars believe that while Christianity may have become the more dominant religion in Europe during this period, Norse Paganism survived as it always has; as an oral culture passed down by elders. Some Christians rejected their beliefs in Norse Paganism, but kept the stories that are more familiar to us in modern times.

Snorri Sturluson, a cultural historian and mythographer, was one of the more well-known individuals who became involved in reviving Norse Paganism. This new form of Paganism was known as 'cultural paganism', as it used parts of pre-Christian Norse Paganism to adapt to the new Chritstian cultural and social contexts. Essentially, Norse Paganism has outlasted the active worship and belief in its gods, while remnants of its rituals have remained for centuries after Christianity became the dominant religion of Scandinavia.

## In Summary

While the history and origins of Norse Paganism are not as detailed as one would like, the available information allows us to understand that Norse Paganism was a belief system that was incorporated into everyday life. It changed and evolved alongside its followers and could be practiced even when other belief systems were introduced. It evolved as languages do, but its foundation, essential beliefs, and values remained constant.

# CHAPTER 2
# NORSE PAGAN BELIEFS AND VALUES

Just as with any other religion, the Norse Pagans had their own beliefs and values. However, there were slight differences between Norse Paganism and other religions. This resulted from the influence of the environment in which they lived, the people they interacted with when they traded goods, the Norse Pagan pathway (belief system) that they followed, as well as the influence of the values of the people that led their regions, such as a royal family or chieftain. While differences were present in the types of beliefs held by a Norse Pagan community, there were common elements that did not change. Key elements of their beliefs and values remained consistent.

## Norse Pagan Beliefs

While the beliefs of Norse Pagans differed slightly depending on where they lived, and who they interacted with, there were common key elements between the beliefs of the various Norse Pagans. These elements remained present, even though they had little to no contact with the tribes that had branched off. These key elements are present even in modern day Norse Pagan pathways, such as Ásatrú and Heathenism.

***The Key Elements of Norse Pagan Beliefs***
Norse Pagan beliefs have six common elements that remain present, no matter which pathway

is followed. This resulted from the fact that Norse Paganism is much more a way of living than it is a religion. The key elements are as follows:

## Norse Paganism Is a Polytheistic Religion

The Norse Pagans worshiped more than one god and/or goddess. They believed that their gods each had unique human characteristics, including a personality, human emotions, talents, and flaws. There are many Norse Pagan gods; their gods could marry and have children. The type of god that was worshiped or celebrated depended on the region you lived in, your social class, as well as what the god stood for (such as good fortune or wisdom). A person could devote themselves to many gods, or only to a single god. Those who devoted themselves to a single god or goddess were called *fulltrúir,* or *vinr*. These words meant 'confidant' or 'friend'.

## Ancestor Worship

As an agricultural community, family was important to the Norse people. As such, they would celebrate their ancestors as deities. These celebrations of worship helped them stay in contact with their loved ones, and were intended to bring prosperity, happiness, and blessings to their family, in order to ensure their well-being. This form of worship took place during a private religious practice in one's community or farmstead. If you did not properly worship your ancestors, it was believed that you would experience bad fortune, and would be haunted by the dead. This type of worship was common among the Finno-Ugric people and the Sámi people.

## Animistic Worldview

It has already been mentioned that Norse Paganism was a way of life for the Norse people.

This meant that they did not separate their culture from their religion. The divine was believed to be a part of everyday life. They believed that they were constantly interacting with their gods and goddesses, spirits, and magical entities as they went about their day. Divinity was present in animals, nature, and even man-made creations, such as their homes. By interacting with this divinity in daily life, a relationship of collaboration was created that benefited both the community members and their world.

**Fate**

You may be familiar with the idea of Fate from Greek mythology. The Norse people had similar beliefs. They believed that the Norns, three magical entities, were responsible for controlling the fate of gods, men, and everything else in the world. However, the Norse people also believed that a person played an active role in their lives. This means that you should not surrender to your circumstances; instead, approach every event or circumstance like a battle that should be fought and confronted with honor.

## Cosmology

Cosmology refers to how the Norse Pagans understood their place in the universe. It encompasses their belief in the gods and goddesses, other magical beings and creatures, the creation of the universe, the afterlife, and the end of the world, Ragnarök. These topics will be covered in detail later in the book.

## The Afterlife

Norse Pagans did not believe that life ended with death. To them, death was only the end of your physical life, while your spirit would continue to live in a new realm. This is one of the reasons why they celebrated their ancestors. They did not believe that you would be sent to a specific realm after death based on your moral concerns so that you could be rewarded or punished. Instead, their beliefs had more to do with *where* you died.

The worship of their ancestors was tied to the fact that the Norse Pagans believed in reincarnation. More specifically, one would be reincarnated into their family line. This is one of the reasons why a newborn would often be named after a deceased family member. The Norse believed that this would allow the family member to be reincarnated through the child.

Those who died in battle were called *Einherjar*. Half of these warriors would go to Odin's Hall, known as Valhalla, where they would wait for the arrival of Ragnarök to fight alongside the Aesir gods. The other half would go to Freyja's hall, called Fólkfangr. Those who died from disease and old age would go to Hel. *Hell* and

*Hel* are not the same. Hel was seen as a place where you could rest and enjoy peace from the labors of your life. If you died at sea, you would live in the Halls of Aegir and Ran. These halls were found deep beneath the waves of the ocean.

## Norse Pagan Values

The values of the Norse Pagans are found in the practices of the Norse Pagan pathway known as Ásatrú. This pathway is the closest to the original form of Norse Paganism practiced by the ancient Norse people, allowing us to derive the values of the Norse Pagans from the *Nine Noble Virtues of Ásatrú*. This pathway focused on the worship of the Aesir gods, who were deities of social realities such as justice and wisdom. Further explanation of who these gods were will be discussed in future chapters.

The virtues set out below are the ethical

standards that were followed by the Norse Pagans. These values, or virtues, were derived from the following Norse literary texts: the *Hávamál*, the *Poetic Edda*, the *Prose Edda*, and other Icelandic sagas. These values were used by the Norse Pagans to determine whether their behavior was appropriate and honorable in whatever situation they found themselves in.

### *The Nine Noble Virtues of Ásatrú*
**Courage**

To the Norse Pagans who follow the pathway of Ásatrú, courage encompasses both physical and moral courage. To them, courage does not mean getting into fights even if you aren't sure you will win. Courage is standing up for what you believe to be right, even if no one else stands beside you. It is fighting for what is right and just, even if it is not the popular opinion of those in your community.

## Truth

Truth is divided into both spiritual and factual truth. It reminds a person to speak what they know to be the truth about something, instead of talking only about what others would like to hear.

## Honor

Honor is your reputation and your moral compass. It is significant to your daily life, as it reminds you that the person you are today will be remembered long after your death. Your deeds, words, and reputation will outlive your physical life.

## Fidelity

Fidelity is your ability to remain true to your gods, kinsmen, spouse, and your community. By betraying your fidelity to these people, you are betraying your community and what they stand for.

## Discipline

To uphold the *Nine Noble Virtues,* you need mental discipline. This discipline will help you to uphold the other virtues. The decision to uphold them is an active choice that you make. It allows you to demonstrate your courage, loyalty, and sense of self-reliance when you face personal challenges.

## Hospitality

Hospitality is not only food, shelter, companionship, and safety. In a Norse Pagan community, hospitality means more than the provision of food, shelter, and companionship. It was granting your guests protection while they lived under your roof after they had eaten at your table.

## Industriousness

The Norse people believed that hard work was,

and is, important in achieving your goals. The work that you put in is owed not only to yourself, but also to your family, community, and the gods.

## Self-Reliance

To thrive as an individual in a thriving community, you need to be able to take care of yourself. While the Norse Pagans believed it was important to honor your gods, it was just as important to take care of your mind and body. The pathway of Ásatrú works to find a balance between doing things for others and yourself.

## Perseverance

This virtue reminds you that you should continue pushing forwards despite the possibility that you could encounter obstacles. When you rise after being defeated, you give yourself the opportunity to learn and grow from your mistakes.

## In Summary

While there are differences between the beliefs and virtues of the different pathways of Norse Paganism, the common elements provide the Norse Pagans with the opportunity to improve their daily lives and their interactions with others, their gods, and nature. Norse Pagan beliefs and values were, and still are, their way of living a fulfilling life. It guided them to do better, to learn and grow, and to stand up for what they believed to be right.

# CHAPTER 3
# SPIRITUAL PRACTICES

The spiritual practices of the Norse Pagans were intended to secure the survival (and regeneration) of their community. As the Norse communities branched off to live in different parts of Northern Europe, their spiritual practices began to diverge from their original practices. Each community celebrated similar rituals and festivals, however, how they celebrated them differed. The differences were dependent on the type of gods being worshiped, the location of the community, and what they required to survive in the future. Spiritual practices and rituals included the celebration of births, naming newborns, funerals, marriages, and the celebration of successful harvests. The agricultural nature of Norse communities meant that their spiritual practices often coincided with the phases of the moon, as they were important when it came to the farming season. The rituals involved in Old Norse spiritual practices often took the form of artifact offerings or depositions, blood sacrifices, and feasts.

These rituals were conducted with a specific intention in mind. They were the Norse Pagans' way of asking their gods for a successful harvest, to bless a child or a battle, or to ask for favorable winds before a long sea voyage. The offering or deposition of artifacts included items such as bracelets, weapons, or tools. These items were placed in (or around) sacred spaces. Sacred spaces included open-air altars, stone altars, and enclosed temples. There were three main types of rituals involved in Norse Pagan spiritual practices.

## The Way of Fire and Ice

The way of fire and ice refers to a radical form of Norse Paganism, as well as the first section of the Norse Pagan creation myth. Their creation myth will be discussed in detail in Chapter 5. The way of fire and ice is a phrase that is used to describe a living tradition that is followed by the modern Norse Pagan community to develop a spirituality that is full of meaning, while they also fulfill their regular needs. This form of Norse Paganism was developed by using the original, meaningful spirituality that is the essence of Norse Paganism. It is similar to the original form of Norse Paganism, as well as bearing many similarities to other Norse Pagan pathways. It allows its practitioners to gain the guidance they need to deal with the challenges that they face in a just and effective manner.

However, it also preaches that its practitioners should not wield the power that they have to hurt or take advantage of others. Every person—no matter their race, religion, or culture—should be treated with dignity and respect. This also ensures that practitioners are actively participating in their lives (in a physical and spiritual sense) as well as participating in their social communities. Norse Paganism, no matter the pathway that is followed, is a part of every aspect of life. Norse Pagans of every pathway believe that the only thing that you can be certain about in life is the process of life, death, and change. As such, you should live your spiritual and physical life in a way that is just, fulfilling, and allows you to engage with your community and environment positively. The activities that they use to engage with their environment, community, and the deities they worship are known as spiritual practices.

Spiritual practices take the form of rituals, festivals, and ceremonies.

## The Types of Rituals Involved in Spiritual Practices

Norse Pagan spiritual practices involve a system of beliefs and customs that are related to each other, but differ depending on the geography and needs of the community. Certain aspects of Old Norse Religion can be generalized—such as the importance of sacred acts and ritual practice. Norse Paganism centered around what you did, and not what you believed. Their rituals were interwoven with their daily lives. Their spiritual practices involved both large community events and smaller, private family rites that took place in their homes. The Norse Pagans believed it was the sacrifices, offerings, and rituals that they performed which brought them blessings of strength, protection, and luck.

## *Three Common Rituals*

### **Sacrifice**

Sacrifices were the primary spiritual practice of the Norse Pagans. These sacrifices, or Blóts, were obligatory. Animal sacrifice was their main type of blood sacrifice. After the ritual killing of the animal, its blood would be sprinkled on the altars dedicated to the gods; and on the inside and outside walls of the designated temple. After the sacrifice was completed, the chieftain of a community would host a feast. During the feast, a ritual toast occurred. It involved the members of the community passing food and drink over the fires that they made to consecrate it. The chieftain would make a ritual gesture once the food and drink had passed through the fire.

Blood sacrifices occurred under many circumstances; during seasonal festivals that were tied to the farming life of a community, before a duel, after a business trade had occurred, at funerals, and directly before setting sail. The idea was that a blood sacrifice to the gods would ensure favorable winds that would ensure that they arrived safely at their destination.

In terms of human sacrifice, the sacrificial killing of a person was done to dedicate their death to either a specific god or a set of gods. It is suggested that the Norse Pagans thought the punishment for a crime should have a sacred meaning. As such, criminals could be "sentenced to sacrifice" as punishment. Sacrifice also took the form of ritual hangings, drownings, and self-sacrifice during times of famine and war. Self-sacrifice during hard times would ensure the survival of community members. In Denmark and Northern Germany, naturally mummified bodies were recovered from peat bogs. Scholars believe that these bodies were human sacrifices.

## Deposition

The deposition of goods is the process of placing a specific item in a certain area, in order to dedicate the deposition to a god. Artifact deposition was practiced in Scandinavia. Items were mainly deposited in and around wetlands. These items included weapons (such as swords, spears, and shields), tools, jewelry, coins, and other materials (or objects) that a community deemed important or associated with a god. While this practice originated in Scandinavia, it began to extend to other Norse communities. The precise purpose of artifact deposition is unclear, however, it may have occurred for the same reason as blood sacrifices.

## Rites of Passage

Rites of passage occurred in all Norse communities. How these rites took place differed depending on the community and the type of rite being celebrated. When a child was accepted into a Norse family, water was ritually sprinkled before the child would be named. It was common for a child to be named after a deceased relative. The Norse people believed that this would allow the spirit of the deceased relative to be reborn via the child being welcomed into the family. This ritual was called *ausa vatni*.

Adoption was common in Norse communities. In Norway, the practice of welcoming an adopted child into your family involves the father, followed by the adoptive child, and then all of their relatives, stepping into a specially made leather shoe.

During weddings, a specific rite of passage took place to convey the bride from her birth family to the family of her husband. This rite of passage was called a "bride run", otherwise known as bruðlaup. Brides wore linen veils, or special headdresses, which were associated with the goddess Freyr and the god Thor. These were the gods commonly associated with weddings.

While very little is known about most rites of passage, scholars have a wealth of information regarding the burial rituals of the Norse Pagans. Burial rituals varied considerably. Cremations, inhumations, and ship burials were common among the Norse people. Inhumations involved the burial of a body, while cremation involved the burning of a body until nothing but ash and bone fragments were left behind. In Viking Age Iceland, the dead were buried in pits, wooden coffins, chambers, boats, and stone cists. However, evidence of cremations were found beside funeral pyres. The ashes of the deceased were buried in pits, pots, kegs, or scattered across the ground. The Norse people even had cemeteries. While solitary graves did occur, most of the gravesites were left unmarked. If they were marked, the use of standing stones or burial mounds was used to memorialize those that had died. Cemeteries were common in market towns such as Hedeby and Kaupang.

The deceased were buried with items called 'grave goods'. Grave goods were present in both cremations and inhumation. They commonly consisted of sacrificed animals and items that reflected the social standing of the individual. One's social standing was also reflected in the type of burial that took place after their death. Ship burials indicated that the person that was buried was a part of the more elite social classes.

In the Ylinga Saga, an old Norse literary text, Snorri Sturluson stated that Odin had declared that the dead should be burned on a funeral pyre with their possessions. Burial mounds and memorial stones, however, would only be erected for notable members of society.

In Prose Edda, Odin's son Baldr was burned on a funeral pyre after his death. His funeral pyre was placed on his ship, known as the Hringhorni, and launched to the sea by the giantess Hyrrokkin. Snorri documented these stories after Iceland had undergone Christianization. He used the Skaldic poem Húsdrápa, written by Úlfar Uggason as his source of information.

While the spiritual practices of Norse Pagan communities differed, one commonality is that they were practiced to ensure the survival of the community and the regeneration of their people. The reality of their practices may not be as exciting or gory as those seen in the media, but they were well-intentioned. The Norse people thought of the consequences of their behavior, and what methods were best to seek the blessings of their gods. They respectfully interacted with their environment and valued the safety and regeneration of their community above all else.

# Norse Pagan Sacred Spaces

The information that details the type of sacred spaces used by the Norse Pagans, such as altars and temples, is mainly based on archeological findings and the research of scholars. A lack of written texts dating from before the Christianization of Northern Europe has left us with little information detailing the types of altars and temples used by the Norse Pagans, as well as what they looked like.

## *The Primary Types of Sacred Spaces*
### Outdoor Spaces

Primarily, the Norse Pagans would practice their spiritual rituals outdoors. Their environment was thought to play a significant role in their ritual practices. Outdoor sacred spaces were known as Vé, meaning "sacred space" or sanctuary. Open-air altars that took the form of a stone pile upon which offerings were made were called *Hörgr,* or stone altars.

Archaeological evidence has shown that the Norse people would deposit artifacts around a specific tree in a grove. Scholars believe that the tree around which such offerings were made was representative of the World Tree, known as Yggdrasil, from Norse mythology. The types of artifacts deposited included beads, weapons, tools, and bones.

**Bodies of Water**
There is archeological evidence of artifact deposition occurring near bodies of water. Bodies of water—such as peat bogs, wetlands, lakes, and rivers—were considered sacred. Artifact deposition near a body of water is

believed to have originated from the story where Odin looked into the well of Mimir to gain divine knowledge.

## Natural Sites

Certain natural sites were designated as areas of importance by the Norse people. These sacred spaces had no permanent structures as designated markings. Instead, they would use standing stones, ditches, or any natural part of the landscape to indicate these specific spaces. Natural features in the environment of the Norse people were sacred to them because they held their environment in high esteem. In Iceland's Snæfellsness Peninsula, a rocky outcrop known as Helgafell can be found. This was considered a sacred space where a small temple was built to worship Thor.

## Temples

Sometimes physical walls were used to protect

sacred spaces. These spaces took on the form of a temple. While physical boundaries were not always four walls and a roof, the Norse intended to enclose sacred spaces. Enclosed spaces allowed for the private worship of, and consultation with, the divine. Temples would also be used to perform sacrifices during the midsummer and midwinter solstices. One famous Norse temple can be found in Uppsala, Sweden. A description of the temple was written by Adam of Bremen in 1070. The temple was supposedly made entirely from gold, and the center hall had statues depicting Odin, Thor, and Freyr. While archeologists have been able to support his claims, little archaeological evidence has been found to provide more information about this temple.

When spiritual spaces took a more physical form, their size would depend on their purpose. Large temples were used to host community celebrations, feasts, and sacrifices. Small religious buildings were separated from these larger halls. They were used for more specific ritual purposes. These rituals may have also included private ritual practices.

In Iceland in 2015, members of the Norse Pagan pathway Ásatrú built the first non-Christian temple in 1,000 years. This temple is called a *Hof*. It was built for the purpose of hosting marriages, feasts, seasonal festivals, coming of age ceremonies, and other Norse Pagan spiritual practices.

## Norse Pagan Festivals That Are Still Celebrated Today

The Norse Pagans based their festivals and feasts on the agricultural nature of their community. This means that they would have had a feast to celebrate the beginning and end of the harvest and planting seasons, and a feast corresponding with each change in the seasons.

They would take these times to make offerings and sacrifices to their gods. The festivals that were celebrated by the original Norse Pagans have changed over the years, in line with the changes in their environment and farming practices. The trade allowed the Norse people to meet new people and interact with different cultures. These interactions allowed for the introduction of new elements into their belief system, which, in turn, caused changes in their celebrations. For example, the introduction of Christianity resulted in the Norse Pagan festival of Ostara becoming what is now known as Easter. Norse Pagan festivals may look different, but they are still present in our modern-day festivals and celebrations.

There is surviving knowledge that has been passed on orally from the Norse Pagans of the Viking Age. Our knowledge of Norse Pagan festivals and spiritual practices originates mainly from this time period. While many festivals that were celebrated by the Vikings are also celebrated today, the festivals that follow are the main festivals that were, and still are, celebrated by the Norse Pagans.

## *Types of Festivals*
### Jul, December 20-31

The Norse Pagan version of a New Year's celebration festival. It spans 12 nights. This festival recognizes the Norse Pagan belief that everything has to end, but it is also important to recognize and celebrate new beginnings. Norse Pagans would give gifts to their friends and family, feast, and dance in celebration of this festival. In Norse mythology, Odin rides Sleipnir–his eight-legged horse–to lead what is called the *Wild Hunt*. The Wild Hunt is the time of year when magical creatures and beings–including the dead–are believed to be roaming the Earth freely. The unpredictable nature of the weather in the Northern parts of Europe was used as evidence to support this belief.

## Thurseblót, January's Full Moon

This festival honors Thor, the god of thunder. Thor was seen as a protector of humanity by the Norse Pagans. The mythology says that Thor would use his powers to drive off the frost giants, called Jötunn. By driving off these giants, the stormy weather would also leave, allowing for the return of spring.

## Disting, February 4

This festival was used to celebrate a person's wealth and new beginnings. It took place at the start of spring. The Norse Pagans would prepare their lands for planting, count their cattle, and their wealth. If a calf was born during this time, the Norse Pagans believed that their year would be prosperous.

## Valisblót, February 14

This feast is a modern Ásatrú festival that

celebrates Vali, the son of Odin. During this festival, Norse Pagans would make offerings to Vali in hope that they would receive his blessings.

## Ostara, March 20-21

This festival celebrates springtime and the renewal of life that accompanies this season. It also celebrates the renewal of the Earth and fertility. It encourages the Norse Pagans to rejoice in it. The festival is named after the heathen Germanic goddess, Ostara, who embodies spring and the renewal of life. The rabbit is the symbol of this festival as it represents fertility. This festival has become what is now known as Easter.

## Walpurgis, April 22 - May 1

Nine nights of revelry and darkness are celebrated to remember and celebrate Odin's sacrifice. Odin hung himself from the tree of life for nine days and nine nights. He was blessed with the knowledge of the runes on the ninth night. This festival represents the extinguishing of the light from the world upon his death so that chaos can roam. The light returns after midnight on the ninth night. It is also when the Wild Hunt finally comes to an end. On May 1, the festival of *Thrimilci* is celebrated to welcome summer.

### Einherjar, May 30

This is a modern-day Ásatrú festival that celebrities the warriors who have fallen in battle and been welcomed into Valhalla.

### Sigurdsblót, June 9

Sigurd was a Norse mythological hero who slew the dragon, Fafnir, to win back the treasure of Rhine. This festival celebrates Sigurd and his heroic deeds.

## Midsummer, June 20-21

The summer solstice is the time of year when the sun is at its highest point. This is when the longest day and the shortest night occur. From now on, the days will start to become shorter, and the nights become longer. It is a festival that celebrates power and activity. As such, the majority of the Norse peoples' trade occurred during this period.

## Lithasblót, July 31 - August 1

A harvest festival that is used to thank the goddess Urda for her bounty and a successful harvest. This festival was also associated with ceremonial magic. Traditionally, Norse Pagans would gift their friends and family with a loaf of bread that had been specially made into the shape of a sun wheel.

## Mabon, September 22-23

The Norse Pagans usually waited to celebrate

this minor festival with Winternights. This festival acknowledged the end of their harvest season and was mainly associated with the making of mead.

## Winternights, October 29 - November 2

This festival marked the end of the summer season and recognized the beginning of the winter season in Northern Europe. During this period of celebration, the Norse Pagans would remember and venerate their ancestors, spirits of the land, the Vanir gods, wisdom, and death. They would also toast to great deeds and tell old tales and legends. The Norse Pagans would stop trading and begin to prepare for the hunting season. This season also marked the beginning of indoor work, craftsmanship, and contemplation. It was the time of year when divination practices and magic would occur.

# CHAPTER 4
# THE POETTIC EDDA
# AND THE PROSE EDDA

While the Norse people had an oral culture, a collection of literary works were compiled at various stages of their history. These works consisted of poems and records of actual events, as well as stories of adventure. Most of these works were compiled after the Christianisation of Scandinavia. Therefore, certain works have to be carefully reviewed for a Christian influence. Scholars have been able to use the few available literary works to learn about the Norse People, their beliefs, culture, religious practices, history, and mythology. The literary works usually take one of two forms: an edda—which is a collection of poetry; or a saga—which mainly contains stories, records, and songs. These works were compiled by historians, scholars, and bards over many years.

## The Eddas

The term "Edda" is used to describe a medieval collection of Icelandic literary works that were compiled from the oral information passed down from the Norse people of the Viking Age. This collection is made up of two known Eddas: the *Poetic Edda* and the *Prose Edda*. Scholars believe that these works were compiled in Iceland in the thirteenth century. As the Eddas date far back into Norse history, the Eddas are used as the main source of information by scholars who are studying the Norse people, their belief systems, and their mythology.

Elements from the *Poetic Edda* can be found in the *Prose Edda*.

## *The Poetic Edda*

The *Poetic Edda* is thought to be the eldest of the two Eddas. As such, it has been named the "Elder Edda" by scholars. Another name for this Edda is the "Sæmundar Edda". The *Poetic Edda* is a poetry collection—called skaldic poetry as the bards who compile the poems are called *Skalds*—that was compiled using a medieval Icelandic manuscript known as the *Codex Regius*. *Codex Regius* translates to "Royal Book", connecting to the fact that the book was stored in the royal library in Copenhagen. While scholars are in disagreement over who the author of this particular Edda is, the information in this Edda has provided them with an abundance of credible information about the Norse people and their beliefs.

The poems contained in this Edda tell the tales of the gods, heroes, and monsters found in Norse mythology. The *Poetic Edda* is believed to have been written in the thirteenth century but its exact whereabouts were unknown until the year 1643. When it was discovered, it first came into Brynólfur Sveinson's possession before the Church of Iceland's Bishop, Skálholt, obtained it.

One of the popular poems found in this Edda is called the "Hávamál". This poem details the story of how Odin hung himself from the branches of Yggdrasil, the world tree, for nine days and nine nights in his quest for knowledge and wisdom. On the ninth night, Odin was blessed with the knowledge of the runic alphabet. This poem is evidence of the Norse Pagans' belief in mysticism and magic.

Even though the author of the *Poetic Edda* is

unknown, it is one of the few comprehensive sources of Germanic legends that is available to scholars. It is detailed and credible enough that it is still used by modern-day scholars to study Norse mythology, their culture, and history. A well-known writer, J.R.R Tolkien, was one such scholar. The *Poetic Edda* inspired him to write the *Lord of the Rings*. If you are familiar with his work, you may find similarities in the information found here. One of these similarities is the parallel between the elven people of Middle Earth and the elves of Norse Mythology.

## The Codex Regius

This manuscript is believed to have been used as one of the pieces of source material for the compilation of the *Poetic Edda*. It was divided into two parts. The first part of the *Codex Regius* contains poetry detailing the creation and destruction of the Nine Realms found in Norse mythology, as well as what the rebirth of this world would look like. The myths detailing the Norse gods and goddesses are also contained in this half of the manuscript.

In the second part of the manuscript, the poetry narrates the legends of Norse heroes and heroines. The first half of this section details 10 songs about the Norse gods and goddesses. In the second half, 19 songs are used to record and celebrate the heroes and heroines.

### *The Prose Edda*

As the *Prose Edda* is seen as the newer Edda, it has become known as the "Younger Edda". The name "Snorri's Edda" is used to refer to its author Snorri Sturluson. Snorri was an Icelandic poet, scholar, and historian, who compiled the *Prose Edda* around 1220 c.e. The mythological stories detailing the histories of the Norse gods are contained in this Edda. Snorri used knowledge of his ancestors—passed down orally to him, the *Poetic Edda,* and the *Codex Regius* to compile his Edda.

Snorri wanted his Edda to be used by Icelandic poets as a manual for Icelandic poetry. The *Prose Edda* can be used by readers to understand the subtleties of alliterative verses in Skaldic poetry. It aims to help readers to gain an understanding of the mythological allusions present in this Edda. It is believed that any Icelandic traveling bard would have been familiar with the tales and poems contained in it. The *Prose Edda* has survived in the form of a prologue and the three following books:

- *Gylfaginning:* a detailed account of the Norse mythological world's destruction and rebirth.

- *Skáldskaparmál:* this book detailed a conversation between two gods: Ægir–one of the Norse gods connected with the sea, and Bragi–the skaldic god of poetry.

- *Háttatal:* a detailed demonstration of the verse forms that are used in Norse mythology.

One of the stories found in this Edda is connected to the *Ynglinga Saga*. In this saga, Odin issues laws that state that the dead are to be burned on a pyre with their possessions; and notable men should have burial mounds or memorial stones made to remember them after their deaths. This is witnessed in a story in the Prose Edda that explains how Baldr, son of Odin and god of light, was burned on a pyre on his ship.

## The Sagas

Sagas were compiled to record a variety of heroic stories. Sagas were based on the deeds and actions of the gods, kings, chieftains, and different heroes and heroines, as well as the adventures of well-known families in Northern

Europe. Even in stories of kings and families, the gods often made an appearance, either as a symbol or directly appearing in person. Authors sometimes wrote about their family's ancestors by using the stories that had been passed down to them over many generations. There are four well-known sagas, which read as follows:

### *The Volsunga Saga*

The story of the Volsunga family is the earliest remaining example of epic poetry that dates back to 1000 c.e. The saga details the adventures of various heroes in this family. One of the more famous adventures tells the tale of Sigurd the Dragon Slayer and his lover, Brynhildr. This tale is one of the more popular stories from this saga. Odin is one of the gods who make frequent appearances in this saga.

### *The Laxdaela Saga*

Scholars believe that this saga was written by a

woman in the thirteenth century. It details the story of Keltill Flathose and his descendants, who had departed from Norway to migrate to the Orkney Islands. This saga contains death, vengeance, and religious piety.

## *The Orkneyinga Saga*

This saga was compiled from a variety of sources and details the history of the Earls of Orkney. These stories introduce several historical, legendary characters. One such story details the conquest of the Orkney Islands by King Harald of Norway.

## *Heimskringla*

This book contains a collection of sagas that were written by Snorri Sturluson. These sagas detailed the Swedish and Norwegian kings. Snorri used sources from the King's sagas, which included *Morkinskinna* and *Fayrskinna*, the twelfth-century Norwegian synoptic histories and oral traditions, as well as notable Skaldic poems to compile this collection. One such saga includes the *Ynglinga Saga*. It is found in the first section of this book, and it details the histories of old Norse kings from as far back as 1177.

# The Literary Texts in the Modern World

## *The Poetic Edda and the Prose Edda*

The *Poetic Edda* and the P*rose Edda* have been translated into English many times over the years. As such, copies of both of these Eddas are available to the public. Many of these books have undergone revisions after being translated by scholars. Scholars have also included explanations of their interpretations of the text, as well as the context in which the information has been translated.

### *The Sagas*

Many of the sagas are housed in the Icelandic Literature Center. Their preservation and protection of these sagas have resulted in Iceland becoming one of the European countries well-known for preserving Norse Paganism as both a culture and a religion. It has allowed scholars to further their study of Norse Paganism and mythology, with the express purpose of obtaining a better understanding of how the ancient Norse communities lived and interacted with each other, and with other communities.

## In Summary

The preservation of literary texts is important in any society. While the ancient Norse people had an oral culture, their lives, beliefs, and lessons learned have been preserved through stories and poetry written by their descendants. This preservation of their lives helps us to gain an understanding of how they lived, in both a physical and spiritual sense. These texts also serve as a means of preserving the important lessons that they learned over many generations, in order to ensure that we do not repeat their mistakes. The literary texts allow the descendants of the Norse people to gain some understanding of where they came from and how they may have come to exist in the universe.

# CHAPTER 5
# THE NORSE PAGAN CREATION MYTH

Like most religions, the Norse Pagans had their own creation myth. Some scholars believe that the Norse Pagan creation myth was created in response to the Christian creation myth after Christianity was introduced to Northern Europe. However, the study of the available Norse literary texts, alongside a study of the oral culture of the Norse Pagans, has revealed many static elements that have remained unchanged for centuries. This has led many scholars to re-evaluate what they know about Norse Paganism. The continued presence of common elements from the texts, and in the oral culture that is still sharing the Norse Pagans' knowledge, has led to the conclusion that the Norse Pagan creation myth that we know today is relatively unchanged from the original creation myth believed by the ancient Norse people.

## Cosmology

Cosmology was used by the Norse Pagans to understand their place in the universe. It encompassed four elements of Norse Paganism: the creation myth, the nine realms, the gods and goddesses, and Ragnarök. In Chapters 5 to 8, we will look at the elements of cosmology in detail.

The Norse Pagan creation myth is the first element of Norse cosmology. It was used by the Norse Pagans to understand how the universe, the Earth, and life were created. The creation myth that is studied today was compiled using the few remaining literary works of the Medieval era, including the *Poetic Edda* and the *Prose Edda*. Interestingly, scholars believe that the elements of the Norse Pagan creation myth studied in the present are nearly identical to the original elements of the creation myth that the original Norse Pagans believed in.

There are elements in Norse Paganism that are similar to elements found in other religions. It is believed that this commonality indicates that Norse Paganism, along with Greek mythology and Egyptian mythology, shares an Indo-European origin. Indo-European is a term that is used to refer to a family of languages, and their subsequent branches, which originated in Europe and Asia.

There are far too many common elements

between these religions and mythologies to list them all in this book. However, some of these common elements include the similarities between the Norse Pagan primordial cow, Audhumbla, and the Egyptian goddess Hathor, who has been depicted with the head of a cow. The cow goddess is present in many Indo-European religions. Parallels are also present in the origin stories of certain gods, such as Greek mythology's Zeus, who was nourished by a goat when he was a baby. This parallels the Norse creation myth where Ymir, the first giant, was nourished by Audhumbla's milk. Many other similarities exist between these two mythologies.

## The Creation of the World

Before the existence of the nine realms, there was a void. This void was called Ginnungagap, or the "Yawning Void". The void was surrounded on either side by two realms. Their environments were polar opposites of one another. Muspelheim was a realm known for its hot, fiery nature and harsh environment. No water existed in this realm. Niflheim, however, was its complete opposite. This realm encompassed the remaining side of Ginnungagap. Its environment was equally harsh, with cold, frigid weather that meant that any water was turned to ice and/or mist. This first bit of existence was called the *world of fire and ice* by the Norse Pagans.

The fact that heat rises is a universal constant, and this is true, too, in Norse mythology. The flames from Muspelheim created a heat that rose to melt the ice in Niflheim, creating water droplets. The droplets drifted away from their home to meet the flames of Muspelheim in Ginnungagap. Their meeting created the sparks that would bring life to the universe.

The first life created was that of the first giant named Ymir, father of the frost giants. Ymir was a hermaphrodite, meaning that he had both male and female reproductive organs. Then, Audhumbla, the primordial cow, came into being. Audhumbla kept Ymir nourished with her milk, while she licked the salt off of the icy rocks in Niflheim to nourish herself.

Her licking eventually began to shape the ice. Audhumbla's licking shaped the ice into the shape of what would become a god named Búri, the grandfather of the Aesir gods. Around the same time, Ymir's sweat formed into a man and a woman underneath his left arm.

Búri had a son that he named Borr, who married a woman named Bestla. Bestla has been described as being Ymir's daughter in some versions of the creation myth, while in others, she is Borr's sister. Either way, Borr and Bestla had three sons together, named Odin, Vili, and Vé.

Their lives were far from perfect, or even pleasant. Ymir and the frost giants that he had created mistreated Odin and his family, making them work long and hard while the giants reaped the benefits. Odin, Vili, and Vé eventually decided that they had had enough. They began to plot how they would kill Ymir. The three brothers eventually succeeded in their plans to kill Ymir, and Ymir's blood drowned nearly all the frost giants, killing them. Bergelmir was the only frost giant to survive.

Odin and his brothers decided to leave Ymir's body in the Ginnungagap. They had decided that they would use his death to create a new world. Out of his flesh, the three brothers created the Earth. Ymir's blood formed the seas, and his skull became the sky. The trio used

Ymir's bones to create the mountains, and his hair to form the trees. They named their new world Midgard. Midgard also means "Middle Enclosure" or "Middle Yard".

The three brothers were pleased with the world that they had created, and they decided that they should also create beings to live here. From the roots and branches of the trees, they carved two forms, a man and a woman. They breathed life into them and named them Ask and Embla, the first human beings.

An ash tree grew from Ymir's body. This tree was called Yggdrasil or the "World Tree". Yggdrasil's branches simultaneously cover the world and support the universe. Each of its roots stretches all the way to one of the three levels of the world. The first root goes to Asgard, the home of the Aesir gods. The second root goes to Jötunnheim, the home of the giants. The third root goes to Niflheim, the primeval world of ice and darkness. A special spring provides each root with water.

In Jötunnheim's spring, the god Mimir gives wisdom. In Niflheim, spring nourishes the adder, Niddhogge, who gnaws at the roots of Yggdrasil. In Asgard's spring, its root is cared for by the three Norn goddesses of fate: Urdu (the past), Verdandi (the present), and Skuld (the future).

Odin, Vili, and Vé were happy with the world that they had created. There were nine unique realms, each with its own unique environment and beings to call it home. Content and proud with what they had created, Odin and his brothers decided to settle in Asgard, where they would live their lives beside the other Aesir gods, have families, and go on epic adventures.

# Why Understanding the Creation Myth Is Important

Many cultures and religions all over the world have a creation myth. The purpose of the creation myth is to allow those who follow its practices to understand how the universe came into existence, what their place is in the universe, as well as create a foundation for their belief system. This foundation helps Norse Pagans to understand why Yggdrasil is important to the continued existence of life. It helps them to understand that the Norse gods and goddesses often have more than one function so that they can ensure the protection and continued existence of life. As humans, we like to understand where we came from and how things came into existence. The existence of a creation myth allows us to answer that question and satisfy our curiosity. The Norse Pagans believed that everything would also come to an end. The creation myth leads on to what is called *Ragnarök*. Ragnarök is essentially the Norse

Pagan version of the apocalypse, and its purpose is to explain how all life will eventually end.

# CHAPTER 6
# THE NINE REALMS

The second element of Norse Pagan cosmology is the nine realms. The number nine is considered to be one of the magical numbers in Norse Pagan magic. This number is significant, as seen by its reappearance throughout Norse mythology and literature. The nine realms are the second element of Norse cosmology. The number nine is repeated throughout the stories continued in the Edda poems. Odin hung from the branches of Yggdrasil for nine days and nine nights seeking wisdom, Heimdall had nine daughters, and Njord waited for Skadi for nine days. As such, it comes as no surprise that there are nine realms instead of, say, eight or ten.

## An Introduction to Each of the Nine Realms

The nine realms were created from the body of the frost giant, Ymir. The realms are housed in the branches and roots of Yggdrasil, and each realm is unique. Every realm has a different environment and relationship to magic. They are also home to different beings that are uniquely suited to that realm. These beings include benevolent and malevolent creatures, magical beings, gods, giants, and humans. Midgard is one of the realms that is known for being home to more than one creature.

### *Niflheim*
One of the first two realms to come into

existence, Niflheim is cold and dark compared to any other realm. The word "Nifleheim" translates to "the realm of fog and mist", which is an apt descriptor of its hostile environment. It is located in the Northern region of the Ginnungagap. Niflheim is home to *Hvergelmir*, the oldest spring in existence. Hergelmir translates to "bubbling, boiling spring". It is guarded by a giant dragon named Niddhog. Norse Pagans believe that this spring is the origin of all living beings, and when they die, they will return to the spring.

Hvergelmir is believed to be the source of all the cold rivers, including the eleven rivers. This water is called *Élivágar,* and it flows down the mountains to the plains of Ginnungagap where it solidifies to form a dense layer of frost and ice. As Yggdrasil began to grow, the tree stretched one of its largest roots into Niflheim and drew water from Hvergelmir.

## *Muspelheim*

The second realm to come into existence, Muspelheim's environment is hostile in the opposite manner to Niflheim. This bright, hot, flaming world is home to lava, soot, and anything associated with heat. Found to the South of the Ginnungagap, Muspelheim is ruled over by the fire giant, Surtr. Surtr and the Aesir gods are sworn enemies. He will ride out of Muspelheim with his flaming sword to attack Asgard when Ragnarök arrives, turning the world into a flaming inferno.

## *Asgard*

Located in the middle of the world, above Midgard in the heavens, this realm is home to the Aesir gods and goddesses. Odin, chief of the Aesir gods, rules Asgard alongside Frigg, his wife, and queen of the Aesir. Asgard is also home to Valhalla, Odin's hall, where warriors who have fallen honorably in battle live after being carefully chosen by the Valkyries. The warriors will rest here and await Ragnarök's arrival so that they may fight alongside the Aesir gods.

## *Midgard*

Home to humans and various other beings, Midgard is found below Asgard in the middle of the world. Asgard and Midgard are connected via the Bifrost. The Bifrost is a rainbow bridge that allows the gods to easily travel between the two realms. Midgard is surrounded by a large, impassable ocean that is home to Jörmungandr, the Great Midgard Serpent. He is believed to be so big that he can encircle Midgard completely when he puts his tail in his mouth.

## *Jötunnheim*

The home of the giants is known as the Jötnar. The frost giants are another sworn enemy of the

Aesir gods. While they are constantly fighting with each other, the Aesir gods and frost giants are known to occasionally have love affairs. Odin and Thor have been recorded as having affairs with the Jötunn. This realm lies on the outermost shores of the ocean and is made up of rocks, wilderness, and dense forests. There is no fertile land here, so the Jötunn people live off of fish from their rivers and animals that they find in their forests.

Loki is a god that was originally from Jötunnheim, but he was accepted by the Aesir gods. They allowed him to live with them until his punishment. Jötunnheim and Asgard are separated by the river Irving, which never freezes. The stronghold of Utgard is thought of as the giant's version of Asgard. The stronghold is so tall that one cannot see the top. The fortress is covered in blocks of snow and icicles. Inside the stronghold lives the feared Jötunn, King Utgard.

## *Vanaheim*

This realm is home to the Vanir gods. This branch of old gods are masters of sorcery and magic. Alongside these capabilities, the Vanir gods are widely acknowledged for their ability to predict the future. Unfortunately, nothing is known about Vanaheim's location or environment.

## *Alfheim*

This realm is known as the land of the elves. It is located next to Asgard in the heavens. Freyr, a Vanir god, rules over this realm. It is home to the elven people, who are considered to be extremely beautiful. Known as light elves, they are minor gods of fertility and light. They assist and hinder humanity as they see fit. Light elves are known for inspiring poetry, art, and music.

## *Svartalfheim*

This realm is home to the dwarves. Found under rocks, inside caves, and underground, these masters of craftsmanship have given many powerful gifts to the Aesir gods. Until his death, Hreidmar was their king. The word Svartalfheim means "dark fields". The dwarves are thought to be dark elves. The magical ring, Draupnir, and Odin's spear, Gungnir, were crafted by the dwarves of Svartalfheim.


## *Helheim*

This realm is home to the dishonorable dead. The dishonorable dead include thieves, murders, and anyone not deemed brave enough to go to Valhalla or Fólkvangr. Hel, the daughter of Loki, is the ruler of this realm. Helheim is also known as the underworld. It is grim and dark here, making it impossible to feel love or joy. When Ragnarök arrives, Hel will lead the dead to the plains of Vigrid and fight against the Aesir gods.

# Why Is It Important to Understand the Nine Realms?

While we do not have many details on the types of environments in each of these realms, the information that we do have allows us to begin our understanding of the beings that live there. Understanding even the basics of these realms helps us better understand the stories contained in the Norse literary texts. It demonstrates how the realms interact with each other and gives context to the Norse Pagan beliefs and spiritual practices.

# CHAPTER 7
# MYTHOLOGICAL GODS, CREATURES, AND BEINGS

This element of Norse cosmology studies who the Norse Pagan gods and goddesses are, as well as what kind of beings are found in Norse Paganism. There are numerous gods and monsters, making it impossible to discuss every single one of them. However, there are certain gods and creatures that are common among all pathways of Norse Paganism, beings that have been continually mentioned throughout history.

This chapter will discuss the two different pantheons of gods and goddesses. This will include what they are the god of, who their family is, and whether they are an Aesir or Vanir god. In the section covering creatures and beings, the most common respective creatures will be discussed. This summary will include a short description of their appearance, where they are from, and why they were feared or revered by the Norse Pagans.

## The Norse Pagan Gods and Goddesses

The Norse Pagan gods are embedded throughout the history, belief systems, and cultures of Europe. The Norse Pagan gods and goddesses are mainly found in Scandinavian and German folklore. The polytheistic nature of Norse culture means that they worship many different types of gods. Their gods focus on different aspects of life, such as wisdom or magic. Polytheism also means that while their spiritual practices may have a common template for their worship, the types of offerings that they make, and celebrations that take place, will depend on which pantheon the god belongs to and what they are the god of. The Norse Pagan gods and goddesses are divided into the following three groups:

- Aesir: the gods of social realities, such as justice and wisdom.

- Vanir: the gods of sexuality, fertility, and magic.

- Jötunn: the giants, which represent chaos and destruction.

## *The Aesir Gods*

The Aesir gods are the principal gods of Norse Paganism. They are mainly venerated by individuals who follow the pathway of Ásatrú.

These gods and goddesses are also popular in the media and Hollywood movies. The Aesir gods live in the realm of Asgard. They were responsible for creating the cosmos, the world, and as a result, human beings. Their purpose is to bring order to the universe. They are known for their skills as warriors, as well as their accomplishments and riches. As a result, they were mainly venerated by the nobility.

The *Prose Edda, Poetic Edda*, and the *Codex Regius* are our main sources of information on the gods and goddesses. These literary texts mainly focus on the Aesir gods, as they were the main pantheon worshiped by the Norse people. These texts provide information on who the gods were, what they accomplished, their families, and their histories.

**Odin**
The Aesir god of war, poetry, wisdom, and

death. He is recognized as the king or chief of the Aesir gods. Odin has an unyielding nature that has supported his quest to gain all the knowledge that he could, in order to understand the world that we live in. He sacrificed his one eye for knowledge, and he hung from Yggdrasil's branches for nine days and nine nights to obtain the runic alphabet. Odin's spear, named Gungnir, is famed for never missing its target. Odin is associated with two ravens, a wolf, and the Valkyries. He and the Valkyries decide which fallen warriors are worthy of joining them in Valhalla.

**Frigg**

The Aesir goddess of love and fertility. She is the queen of the Aesir gods and Odin's wife. She is said to have the power of divination that gives her an air of mystery. Frigg is a protective mother who loved her son Balder so much that she took an oath from the elements, facing beasts, weapons, and poisons. This promise ensured that they would not harm her son.

## Balder

The god of light. Balder is an Aesir god. He is the son of Frigg and Odin. While he was believed to have been immortal, he was killed by a bough of mistletoe. Mistletoe, an element exempt from Frigg's oath, held both his life and death. He will return to the world upon its rebirth after Ragnarök. As such, the Norse Pagans have connected Balder with the cycle of death and rebirth. Balder was believed to have been beautifully radiant, fair, and kind. He was killed by his blind brother, Hod, who had been tricked by Loki.

## Loki

The god of mischief, trickery, and thieves. He may have come from Jötunnheim, but he is classified as an Aesir god. He used his skills in trickery and mischief to trick Hod into killing

Balder. He is married to Sigyn, whose origins as either an Aesir or Vanir goddess are unknown.

## Hod

The blind Aesir god of winter. Hod is the son of Odin, and he is Balder and Vali's brother. He was tricked by Loki and ended up killing Balder by throwing a bough of mistletoe at him.

## Vali

It is known that he is an Aesir god, however, the only other information that scholars have of Vali is that he is Odin's son and brother to Hod and Balder. He avenges Balder's death by killing Hod.

## Thor

Thor is the protector of humanity and the Aesir god of thunder. He wields the hammer Mjölnir. Thor is known for his bravery, strength, healing abilities, and righteousness among the Aesir gods. Thor is also considered to be a god of agriculture, as he was believed to be able to bring the rains that were needed in times of drought. Offerings were made to Thor to gain his favor by the Norse agricultural communities.

## Tyr

Tyr is the Aesir god of war, heroic victory, and triumph. Tyr sacrificed his hand to capture and chain Fenrir, making him left-handed.

## Heimdall

The Aesir god of light. Heimdall is on constant alert, protecting Asgard against any possible attacks. He is known as the guardian of the gods as a result. Like Balder and Vali, he is one of Odin's sons. Heimdall has nine daughters.

## Hel

The Aesir goddess of the underworld. Hel is Loki's daughter, and she is the sister of Fenrir and Jörgmungandr. She was sent by Odin to preside over the realm of Helheim. Hel is said to look death-like.

### *The Vanir Gods*

The Vanir gods that are known are mainly the gods who joined the Aesir pantheon, but the Vanir gods were a different type of god from the Aesir. Very little is known about the Vanir gods and goddesses. These Earth-based gods possessed knowledge and skills pertaining to fate-based magic called *seiðr*. They represented prosperity, peace, and fertility. The Vanir gods are suited to individual worship and were favored by the common people because they were mainly concerned with ensuring that the land is fertile, providing food, and protecting the young and weak. Many scholars think that the Vanir benefited from peace, fair weather, and the type of wealth that normally passes through a community. While they may not have been warriors, their magic put them on equal footing with the Aesir gods when it came to defending themselves. The main Vanir gods are Njord and his two children, Freyr and Freya.

## Njord

The Vanir god of the sea. He was the leader of the Vanir before he went to live in Asgard. Njord is associated with bringing a good bounty to fishermen and protecting ships at sea if they are carrying gold and other valuables. He is the father of the Vanir god Freyr, as well as the Vanir goddess Freya.

## Freyr

The Vanir god of fertility. Freyr is a symbol of prosperity and pleasant weather. He is thought to be the kindest and noblest of all the gods. As such, he is the most sacred and respected Vanir god.

## Freya

The Vanir goddess of beauty and femininity. She is a passionate goddess who is also sensual. This resulted in her being associated with love, fertility, and beauty. Freya introduced seiðr magic to the Aesir gods. Freya bestows prosperity on the land and the sea.

## Njord's Sister

Njord's sister was an unnamed goddess believed to be the mother of Freyr and Freya.

## Aegir

The Vanir god of shipwrecks and drowning.

## *The Aesir-Vanir War*

Originally, the Aesir and the Vanir were two separate pantheons of gods. While this event is important to Norse mythology, there is much discourse surrounding both the cause and events of this war. Textual accounts only give us a vague idea of what may have occurred between the two pantheons, as well as what led to their unification into the pantheon that is well-known today. The information concerning the Aesir-Vanir war is fragmented between a poem in the *Poetic Edda*, called the *Völuspa*, a book in the *Prose Edda* known as the *Skáldskaparmál*, as well as the *Ynglinga Saga* that is found in the *Heimskringla*.

Scholars believe that the Vanir were originally more popular among the Norse Pagans and received more tributes and offerings than the Aesir. The Aesir gods were upset by this, possibly even jealous. The exact cause that led to the two pantheons fighting a war is unknown. It is known that while the Aesir gods were highly-skilled fighters, the Vanir gods were skilled with magic, which helped put their fighting prowess on equal footing with the Aesir. This equality between their skill sets means that there was immense damage suffered by both sides. Eventually, they decided to call a truce. The truce involved an exchange of members from each pantheon. Njord and his two children, Freyr and Freya of the Vanir, went to live in Asgard and became members of the Aesir. Hoenir and Mimir of the Aesir went to live in Vanaheim, although their reception was less friendly than that of Njord and his children.

Hoenir was handsome and strong, the Vanir deemed him perfect for replacing their chieftain, Njord. Mimir, a god of wisdom, was chosen to become Hoenir's chief advisor. However, even though Mimir gave Hoenir good advice when they were in private, he often told Hoenir to ask someone else for advice when they were in meetings. Mimir had confidence in Hoenir's ability to make decisions, but the Vanir gods did not know this. Instead, they thought that Mimir was not honorable and that the Aesir gods had cheated them. They killed Mimir and sent his severed head back to Odin. In Asgard, Odin and Freya used seiðr magic to preserve and reanimate Mimir's head. This allowed Mimir to give Odin advice from a well found beside one of Yggdrasil's roots.

Another agreement that formed as part of the truce was that the two pantheons would agree that they were equals. This meant that they would receive the same type, amounts of sacrifices, and amounts of honor from human worshippers. This truce allowed the two pantheons to unite as one pantheon, becoming the group of Norse gods and goddesses that we know today.

## Creatures and Beings

The existence of creatures and beings is common in all cultures. The unknown has always been terrifying to humanity, however, the idea of a creature being responsible for the unexplainable takes away some of the fear. It provides us with a solution or even a way to prevent the bad thing from happening again, giving us some control over the unknown. By teaching your children that an illness or death was caused by a creature, you can teach them what behaviors and situations they should avoid for their physical (or spiritual) safety. It eases the fear of the unknown by giving you ways to cope. You may be familiar with some of the creatures and beings of Norse Paganism, such as the Valkyries and elves.

The existence of creatures and beings in Norse Paganism allowed the Norse people to gain an understanding of changes in their environment. They believed that these beings had to be real because their gods and goddesses had defeated them many times before. Creatures and beings were less powerful than the Norse gods but slightly more powerful than the Norse people. However, this did not deter the Norse, because they had the gods to back them up when these creatures decided to cause trouble. Creatures and beings could be good, evil, or both, depending on the circumstances and their mood. In the section that follows, we will discuss the main types of creatures that the Norse Pagans believed in.

### *Dwarves*

Dwarves in Norse mythology are nothing like the small creatures that we are familiar with in children's stories. In fact, Norse mythology never explicitly states that dwarves are small. These human-like creatures are well-known in both Norse and German mythology. They live below the ground, in caves and mountains. This, alongside their pitch-black appearance, has led to them also being known as "Dark Elves". The Norse people believed that dwarves evolved from the maggots that were found in Ymir's corpse. The Aesir gods and goddesses gifted them with reason, creating the dwarves that currently exist in Norse mythology. They live in the realm of Svartalfheim. It is believed that Svartalfheim can be found underground. It is said that it takes the shape of a warren of forges.

Dwarves are respected for their skills as master weapons crafters and jewelers in Norse mythology. One of their more famous creations is Mjölnir, Thor's famous hammer. The dwarves also created Gungnir, Odin's spear, which was said to never miss its target. Some of the legends surrounding dwarves say that they live underground because if they are exposed to sunlight, they will turn to stone. One well-known account of this occurring in Norse mythology is when Alviss, a dwarf, claimed the hand of Thor's daughter in marriage. He was tricked into talking until dawn when he was struck with sunlight and turned to stone.

## *Elves*

When you think of elves, you are probably thinking of the tall, elegant beings from J.R.R Tolkien's *Lord of the Rings*. While the Norse version of elves is slightly different, Tolkien did gain his inspiration for his version of the elves from Norse mythology. Typically, two groups of elves are said to exist: the dark elves and the light elves. Norse literature never specified the height of the elves, as such, dwarves are often referred to as the "Dark Elves".

The second group of elves is called "Light Elves". They are incredibly beautiful beings that were considered gods of the Aesir and Vanir. This was connected to the fact that the Vanir god, Freyr, was said to be the ruler of Alfheim, the realm of the elves. Elves cannot be called malevolent or benevolent, as the few records of their interactions with humanity had them both causing and healing illnesses without providing their reasons. The Norse people believed that the elves had children with humans to create children that looked human but possessed incredible power.

## Draugr

These blood-thirsty, zombie-like creatures were believed to bring disease and bad luck to Norse communities. Their decaying bodies smelled awful, and they were able to increase their size if they needed to. Draugr live in their graves so that they can defend the treasures and goods that they were buried with. They escape their tombs by swimming through the rock. They were believed to visit communities and torture those who had wronged them when they were alive. They would enter the person's dreams and torture them through nightmares. In the morning, the person would wake up to a gift, that was left by the Draugr, to let them know that their encounter was real. In order to kill the

Draugr, one would have to dismember their body and set them ablaze. Sometimes, the Draugr's body would be so decayed that they would suffer a second death. The Norse people believed that you were at risk of becoming a Draugr after death if you had been evil, greedy, or unpopular when you were alive. Royal palaces and burial grounds were the common homes of these evil creatures.

## *Mare*

Mare is one of the more terrifying creatures that are found in Norse mythology. Mare was believed to have been responsible for causing bad dreams. It would sit on your chest as you slept and leave tangles in your hair as proof that it had visited. The Norse people believed that Mare was the wandering soul of a living person who would torture innocent people at night. It was thought to be similar to a demon. One of the other versions of this creature is that it was the soul of a witch that would take on the form of an animal. The ancient Norse people believed that your soul could wander at night when you slept. This belief was reflected in a story where Odin said that he was afraid that he would lose his soul because it wandered so much.

### *Hulder or Huldra*

These female entities are responsible for protecting natural locations, such as forests. They are incredibly beautiful and use an illusion to give them the appearance of a normal human woman. In their natural form, a Huldra has hair that resembles that of a cow's tail, and their backs are covered in tree bark. They walk among the people in Norse communities and seduce young men. They lure these young, single men into the forest, where the men either become their slaves or lovers until they are eventually released. The Huldra suck the life essence out of these young men. Once a man has been released from the Huldra, he will lose his temptation to return to her. The only way to break the illusion created by the Huldra is to spot her tail.

## *Kraken*

You may be familiar with this creature from stories about pirates. The Kraken originates in Norse mythology. It is an aquatic sea monster that the Norse people believed to have lived on the coast of Greenland and Norway. The Kraken looks like a gigantic squid-like creature. They are so large that they could be mistaken for an island. If you were to set foot on them, the "island" would sink so that the Kraken could feed upon the prey that it had caught. They generally prey on fish. Their hunting methods included releasing their bowels into the water so that its intense stench would attract the fish. When the Kraken would attack ships, it created a whirlpool as it surfaced, trapping the ships so that it could attack.

### *Ratatoskr*

This troublesome creature looked like a squirrel. He was responsible for delivering messages between the gods and goddesses by running up the branches and roots of Yggdrasil. Ratatoskr would always try to instigate a fight between the wise eagle, that was perched in the branches of Yggdrasil, and the dragon, that sat at the base of Yggdrasil's roots. If these two creatures fought, Yggdrasil would be destroyed by their immense powers.

### *Trolls*

Trolls belong to one of two groups. They were either the large, ugly trolls, which we are familiar with from children's stories, that live in forests and mountains; or they were small-gnome trolls. Small gnome-trolls live in deep caverns. They are malevolent creatures who are known for granting their kindness if you are fortunate enough to gain their favor. Boulders cover the countryside of Scandinavia, and the

Norse Pagans believe that these boulders were either used as weapons by the giants, or they are the trolls who have been turned to stone in the sunlight.

### Norns

We are all familiar with the concept of fate. The Norns were the three goddesses of fate. They were called Urdur (the past), Verdandi (the present), and Skuld (the future). The Norse Pagans believed that you could not change your fate, nor could you deceive the fates into changing it. The Norns were also responsible for caring for the roots of Yggdrasil. They attempted to slow down its inevitable death. However, Norse Pagans believe that everything has to end, that even Yggdrasil will die one day, and the world will end with Ragnarök.

### Valkyries

The Valkyries were noble and elegant female

spirits who helped Odin. They were responsible for choosing the warriors that would live and die in battle. The warriors that were slain that they deemed brave and honorable were brought to Valhalla. The Norse Pagans believed that the Valkyries could use magic to ensure that the outcome of a battle was in their favor.

## *Sleipnir*

This eight-legged horse is a celestial entity. He is the son of Loki. After shape-shifting into a mare, Loki was impregnated by one of the stallions belonging to the giants and bore Sleipnir to life. Sleipnir is a helper spirit ridden by Odin on his journey through Yggdrasil's roots and branches. He carries Odin on his journey across the nine realms. Sleipnir is a symbol of power and greatness in Norse mythology.

## *Fenrir*

The female giant, Angroboda, and the god, Loki,

are parents to the wolf, Fenrir. The Norse people believed that Fenrir aimed to wreak havoc on all of the nine realms. The gods had hoped to dampen his chaotic nature by raising him in Asgard. It did not work, so they decided that they needed to contain him for the safety of the nine realms. The gods told Fenrir that they wanted to play a game with him. They wanted to see how strong Fenrir was by chaining him up and having him attempt to break the chains. Fenrir was intrigued and agreed to play. He broke chain after chain until the last chain was brought out by the gods. This chain, known as Gleipnir, had been specially crafted by the dwarves to be stronger than anything else in the universe. However, at the sight of this last chain, Fenrir began to get suspicious. He asked one of the gods to place their hand in his mouth as a sign of trust. The god Tyr volunteered, aware that he would lose his hand, but he was prepared to do it to protect the realms.

When Fenrir realized he was tricked, he took Tyr's hand. This necessary sacrifice allowed the gods to chain Fenrir to a boulder. They put a sword in Fenrir's mouth to keep it open. The drool that ran out of his mouth at this action is believed to have created the river, Expectation, whose name refers to Ragnarök. When Fenrir finally breaks free of the chains, he will lay his wrath on the gods.

Fenrir is the father of the two wolves, Skoll and Hati. These two wolves are always chasing the sun and the moon so that the days can change to night and vice versa. They will catch the sun and the moon at the end of the world and devour them. Fenrir is the brother of the Midgard serpent, Jörgmungandr, and Hel, the queen of the underworld. He is destined to be one of the most fierce beings in existence. He is destined to kill Odin before he will be killed by Viðarr, one of Odin's sons.

## Jötunn

These frost giants are the sworn enemies of the Aesir gods. They live in the realm of Jötunnheim. The frost giants are described as being both incredibly beautiful and grotesque. While the name giant implies that they are larger than the average human, they have never been described as being larger than the gods or humans. Trolls, Jörgmungandr, and Fenrir are a subset of the Jötunn; while Hel and Ymir are classified as Jötunn.

## Jörmungandr

The Midgard serpent is an enormous snake that lives in Midgard's ocean. He can surround the world. He is famously depicted as biting his tail as he holds up Midgard. Popular motifs of Jörgmungandr include the ouroboros—a circular symbol that represents the cycle of destruction and rebirth. He is Thor's sworn enemy. They have fought several times and are fated to kill each other at Ragnarök.

## *Huginn and Munnin*

These two ravens are a part of Odin's menagerie of spirits. Huginn means thought, while Muninn means mind. The two ravens sit on Odin's shoulder and recite all that they witness into his ears. Every morning they fly across the world to discover information and bring it to him. This is the reason why Odin is strongly linked with ravens. The appearance of ravens after the Norse Pagans make a gift to Odin is said to symbolize his acceptance of the offering. As carrion birds, they are seen as collecting gifts for Odin post-battle. Ravens are very intelligent birds, and their names represent their intelligence.

## *Audhumbla*

The mythical, primordial cow who fed and

nourished Ymir with her milk. Her name translates as "hornless, milk-rich cow". She is known for licking the salt-stone that revealed Búri, the grandfather of the gods. Audhumbla existed at the birth of creation, and helped bring the primary creatures into being.

## *Fylgja and Hamingja*

After a child is born, a spirit animal known as Fylgja will show up to eat the afterbirth. The type of animal that eats the afterbirth is believed to reflect the child's future character. Tame children have a fox as their Fylgja. Children who are wild will have either a wolf, bear, serpent, or eagle appearing as their Fylgja. The appearance of this animal can even refer to the ability to shape-shift between animals.

The female guardian spirit Hamingja, is believed to bring luck and happiness to a person. When the person dies, it is believed that their Hamingja is given to their most cherished family member. The Hamingja will increase this family member's fortune in time. Hamingja may also appear as animals.

## *Heidrun*

A mythical goat who is described in the *Poetic Edda* and the *Prose Edda*. She eats a special bud off a tree that is known as the Laeraðr. This bud allows her to produce enough mead to fill a cauldron every day. Her clear mead provides for the warriors of Valhalla's needs. Her diet of buds has to be carefully controlled to keep her relationship with the tree going so that she can provide for the warriors at the hall.

## *Nidhöggr*

This famous serpent is also known as a "curse-striker". It dwells beneath Yggdrasil and sucks on its roots, hurting the tree and threatening its strength to hold up the nine realms. Nidhöggr wants the cosmos to fall into chaos. At Ragnarök, he will help the Jötunn in the battle against the gods. His appearance in flight is meant to announce the beginning of the end of the world.

### *Tanngrisnir and Tanngnjóstr*

The two goats who pull Thor's chariot. Thor kills his goats every day so that he can eat them. Afterward, he resurrects the two goats with his hammer so that he can have his next daily meal.

# The Importance of Understanding the Gods, Creatures, and Beings in Norse Mythology

While there are many gods, creatures, and beings in Norse mythology, this discussion covers those that are central to the majority of the Norse Pagan pathways. They each play a major role in this belief system and provided the Norse people with a way to explain unknown circumstances and disasters. It helped to satisfy their curiosity and give them a reason behind events they couldn't explain. These gods, creatures, and beings all have a role to play in Norse Paganism. Their roles may differ from each other, but they are important to understand so that the Norse literary texts can be interpreted and understood in the correct context.

# CHAPTER 8
# RAGNARÖK

Ragnarök is a term that has gained popularity in the media in recent years, due to the increase in movies and series inspired by aspects of Norse mythology. Essentially, Ragnarök is the Norse Pagan version of the apocalypse. However, this end of the world prediction is meant to be an epic battle that will see the death and rebirth of the world. It has not happened yet but is an imminent part of the future. This aspect of death and rebirth is important in Norse Pagan cosmology, as they believe that everything must eventually come to an end so that it can be reborn into something new. This aligns with their beliefs in reincarnation. However, there are few written records of what Ragnarök is. There is no specific date or day that tells us when the end will begin; instead, it starts with the crowing of a rooster.

## The End of Days

If Yggdrasil dies, the gods will follow. The end of the world will begin when everything that is seen as a given by the ancient Norse Pagans is destroyed. It won't start with a dramatic bang or any other obvious sign. Small changes will occur first before they begin to increase in an intensity that cannot be ignored.

The end of the world will begin with the crowing of the rooster. His crows will awaken all the members of the nine realms. In Asgard, the Aesir gods will be warned of the impending doom by a rooster with a golden comb atop his head. In Helheim, the frightening sounds of a hellhound will grace the realm.

The people will begin to turn on each other. Conflict and betrayal will be rife throughout the nine realms. A harsh and unrelenting winter will settle over the world, one that is followed by another, equally unrelenting winter. Fenrir's sons, who have been chasing the sun and the moon since they were created, will finally catch up and eat them. The disappearance of the sun and the moon will be followed by the stars fading from existence.

The nine realms will be torn apart by earthquakes. Jörmungandr, the Midgard serpent, will leave his place in the ocean to swim to the battlefield. His journey will cause great floods that will damage the land. Snow will fall and a cold wind will blow constantly through the land. These harsh winters will badly damage the nine realms and their inhabitants.

Surtr, king of Muspelheim, will lead five giants to the battlefield. The battlefield is called *Vigrid*. The gods and humanity will begin to prepare for the looming battle. On the battlefield, broad lines will be drawn between Surtr's forces and the gods. It is said that the battlefield will be bloody and littered with bodies of fallen warriors, gods, and other creatures.

During the battle, Heimdall and Loki will fight until they eventually kill each other. Then Surtr will kill Freyr so that he can engulf the world in fire. Odin will be attacked and killed by Fenrir. Fenrir will be killed by Odin's son Vidar, who wants to avenge the death of his father.

Long-time enemies Thor and Jörmungandr will

battle it out one last time. Thor will manage to kill the great Midgard serpent, however, Jörmungandr gets his revenge before he breathes his last breath, soaking Thor with his venom. Thor will only manage to make it nine steps onto the battlefield before dying.

Many gods will die in this battle, but it is not the end of all things. A period of renewal will fall upon the world after the battle has been fought. The survivors will remake the world and create new lives. The gods who survive include Vidar and Vali–Odin's sons, Frigg, Freya, Idunn, and Thor's children. Baldur will make his way out of the underworld and return to this new world. This new order of gods will return to the place where Asgard once stood and create a new home for themselves. They will remember and honor those who fell during Ragnarök, celebrating their memories and spirits by telling stories of the battle to the new generation of gods.

In Midgard, two humans will emerge from the trees after the battle is over. These humans, Lif and Lifthrasir, will rebuild their lives and repopulate the world. Life will be renewed and carry on once more.

## The Importance of Understanding Ragnarök

The Norse Pagans believe that everything will eventually end, but they believe in a cycle of death, rebirth, and renewal. What this means is that the end of one thing allows you to start something new. In this case, the end of the known world will allow us to create a new world, with new lives, beliefs, and a new pantheon of gods and goddesses. It allows us to grow and learn from our mistakes. Ragnarök is important in helping the world and its inhabitants to embrace change, learn from their past, and forge a new world.

# CHAPTER 9
# MAGIC IN NORSE PAGANISM

When you think of the word Paganism, you probably think it is synonymous with magic. In reality, these two terms are separate. Paganism is a spiritual belief system, while magic is using the energy of the world around you to weave it into your thoughts, words, and physical actions, so that you can create your desired outcome. Magic allows you to access a power that will allow you the opportunity to change yourself, your circumstances, and your future. Norse Pagans do not consider magic to be evil. They even had several gods who they associated specifically with magic. The main gods associated with magic were the Vanir gods, Odin, and Frigg.

It is important to note that magic requires a controlled emotional input. When you conduct ritual magic, your desires must be sincere. You must intend to follow through with what you would like to accomplish. Magic is a way for you to exercise your agency and interact with the spiritual aspects of the world. This interaction takes the form of rituals, practices, and celebrations. In this chapter, we will discuss the types of Norse Pagan magic, as well as the relationship of shamanism to Norse Paganism.

## Norse Pagan Magic and Shamanism

While magic involves working with the energy

around you, shamanism focuses on an individual, called a Shaman. Shamans use a trance-like state to communicate with the spirit world. They would appeal to the spirits for help for either a single person or for their community. Shamanism and magic form a part of mysticism, which is prevalent in Norse Paganism. The Eddic poem *Hávamál* explains how Odin hung from the branches of Yggdrasil for nine days and nine nights. He sacrificed himself so that he could obtain the knowledge of the runes. This also contributed to the number nine becoming one of the sacred numbers of Norse Pagan magic.

Odin's sacrifice resulted in his association with the runes and runic magic. Charms are also associated with runes, however not much is known about the creation of charms in the original version of Norse Paganism. Charms were used to treat issues such as disease in livestock and illness in humans.

Another form of Norse Pagan magic with which Odin was associated is called *seiðr magic*. This type of magic includes divination. Practitioners of seiðr magic were called priestesses, or seiðr workers. They usually came from the Sámi or Finnish people, and, on occasion, were even from the British Isles. This resulted in this form of magic having many similarities to Sámi/Balto-Finnic shamanism. The influence of other cultures on Norse Pagan magic has created different types of magic that were usually dependent on the area in which one lived. Some of these types of magic are still practiced, to a certain degree, in the present.

## The Types of Norse Pagan Magic

### *Spædom*
Spæ means "to speak" in the Old Norse language. It is a magic practice that focuses on prophecy. This type of magic usually forms part

of seiðr magic. It is mainly practiced by women.

## *Seiðr Magic*

Seiðr magic is the main form of Norse Pagan magic practiced in the present. It usually forms part of the Norse Pagan pathway, Ásatrú. The word seiðr means "to seethe". It is an ancient Norse Pagan practice that is associated with prophecy and shaping the future, as such it often includes spæ magic. While not much is known about the original practice, scholars and modern-day Norse Pagans associate modern seiðr magic with practices such as astral journeying, visions, trancework, and other similar spiritual work. As such, seiðr magic has also been called witchcraft.

Seiðr magic is associated with the Vanir goddess, Freya. Scholars believe that Freya is responsible for introducing seiðr magic to the Aesir gods. Seiðr magic was an ancient form of Norse magic that continued into the Medieval and Viking Ages. However, seiðr magic is being revived by modern-day witches. Practitioners of this magic path are mainly women, as it is considered to be a feminine practice. These women were called *Volva*, which was the Norse word for a female witch. Men who practiced this form of magic were called *Seidmann*, but they were usually looked down upon in their communities as it was mainly a feminine practice. Even Odin, who is one of the more well-known practitioners of seiðr magic, was criticized by Loki in the Edda poems for practicing a female occupation.

Pursuing the practice of seiðr magic is a lifelong journey. You have to dedicate yourself to this form of magic. When the Volva was originally called to do their work, their practices used processes that bear many similarities to the type of shamanism found in Siberian culture, which is why seiðr magic is sometimes talked about in the same context as shamanism.

## Practices

Volva would travel between the Norse communities to offer their services. When they partook in rituals meant for prophesying the future, they would enter a trancelike state. A prophecy was meant to clarify the past and present events so that communities could find a better way to move forward in the future. Visionary journeying was a practice that was used to accompany the process of prophecy so that the Volva could interpret what she saw in a specific context. These practices allowed the Volva to speak with the spirits of Helheim. Spirits who resided in Helheim were known for granting insight and wisdom to the Volva.

The Volva were believed to be able to shapeshift. Shapeshifting took on the form of astral projection and dreaming. These practices are being revived by modern-day Norse Pagans, who have decided to go on the journey of seiðr magic. As many original seiðr practices are shrouded in mystery, modern-day witches use the information that is present in the Norse literary texts, alongside archeological evidence, as well as what has been passed down orally through the Norse Pagan communities.

## Tools

Through the study of archaeological evidence, scholars have found that the main tools of the Volva would include a magical staff, herbs, a blue cloak, and charms. Runes would be kept in a special bag on her person, at all times.

## Animal Spirit Guides

Volva would use animal spirit guides to guide them and keep them safe during their spiritual journeys through the realms. The Norse Pagans considered the boar, bear, wolf, raven, horse, cat, dog, eagles, and snakes to be sacred animals. Women who practiced seiðr magic were linked with snakes because they were ambiguous symbols of good and evil.

## *Galdrastafir*

This version of Icelandic magic is also known as "incantation staves". It emerged after the Christianisation of Scandinavia. Norse Pagan practices were combined with Christian mysticism to create a form of ceremonial magic called *Galdrastafir*. It is a Norse-Christian form of socialization and can only be learned from a master by a student, as careful guidance is needed.

## *Trolldom*

Scandinavian folk magic has been practiced for 500 years. It became an isolated practice in the late fourteenth century. Trolldom is passed down through oral traditions and is customarily taught by a master to a student. Trolldom practices include spells for healing, stalling, protection, and luck, as well as divination.

This form of magic is mainly found in Norway and Sweden. Trolldom means "sorcery" in the Swedish language. It is a part of Nordic folklore. Practitioners of this magic are called *Trollkunnings*. Trollkunnings work together to resolve various problems and ailments. Traditionally, the Trollkunning would first conduct a psychic reading to invoke the spirits that may be causing the problem or illness. They would also use various herbs and plants to heal the sick. Trollkunnings were able to perform spellwork and spiritual practices that were detailed in a special book called the "black book". This book contains a collection of spells, rituals, and remedies. Some of these remedies include ground ivy, which was used to heal wounds, ward off colds, and protect against evil entities. They also used willow to soothe anger and dampen conflicts.

Trollkunnings would also be summoned by Norse communities to handle and banish nature spirits. They would also attend to the wounds of the community members attacked by the elvish.

Trolldom was the magic of the folk and as such, it changed as the culture and religions of the people changed. When sixteenth-century Scandinavia had witch hunts, Trolldom practitioners were caught in the argument even though Trolldom was used for good. Practitioners of this magic path were put on trial for "superstition", as Trolldom uses both spiritual and magic-based beliefs and traditions. Fortunately, Trolldom survived the witch trials and remained a recognized profession until the 1950s, when modern medicine and science became commonplace in the media, which led to their widespread use in local communities.

Recently, there has been a renewed interest in alternative and holistic medicine. Trolldom has slowly begun to reappear, but true practitioners are still rare. Its resurrection mainly takes the form of divination techniques, such as rune casting. Rune casting is an ancient method of magic that became dormant after the introduction (and later, acceptance) of the Latin alphabet in Scandinavia. It was re-awakened and incorporated into later Trolldom practices, where modern pagans adopted it into their magic practices. Witches who adopt Trolldom practices intend to become attuned to their subconscious so that they can receive guidance, advice, and predictions of future events.

## The Importance of Understanding the Different Types of Norse Pagan Magic Paths

By learning about the different magic paths that are available to the Norse Pagans, you can make an informed decision about the type of magic that you want to be involved in. It also helps you determine whether you are prepared to go on a lifelong journey, such as in seiðr magic, or whether you are only prepared to introduce small, easier-to-manage aspects of magic into your life. This overview of the types of Norse magic helps determine whether you even want to incorporate magic into your Norse Pagan practices.

# CHAPTER 10
# RUNES, TAROT AND ASTROLOGY

Runes, Tarot and Astrology are all practices found within modern Norse Pagan magic. Historically, runes were the main tools used by seiðr practitioners to gain guidance, answer questions, and conduct their rituals and ceremonies. In modern-day Norse Paganism, tarot and astrology have been introduced and incorporated into Norse Paganism through the influence and contact of other religions and magical pathways. They provide practitioners with a choice. They can either choose a single or combination of tools to use for their practice. These tools allow practitioners to gain guidance about questions that are asked, events and circumstances in which they find themselves, and possible future realities. They help practitioners make a choice that suits them. Runes, tarot, and astrology are used for private practice in the modern world, while in the past, runes were used by the Volva to help their communities.

## Runes

You are probably familiar with runes as symbols that can be used to decorate clothing, jewelry, and weapons to give them a more 'Viking' look. While the Norse Pagans did inscribe runes on weapons, jewelry, and clothing, runes are actually a set of characters that belong to the several alphabets of the Germanic peoples from the third to thirteenth centuries. This ancient alphabet originated in German and Scandinavian countries. Four main runic alphabets developed and evolved over the centuries, mainly Elder Futhark, Younger Futhark, Anglo-Saxon or Anglo-Frisian Futhorc, and the Medieval Futhork.

Runes were used for writing, but they also had a great spiritual significance for the Norse Pagans. Historically, runes were used for both magical and practical purposes. They were used to write commemorative messages on objects, such as tools and jewelry; on runestones, and for charms. It was believed that certain runes could be used to enchant an object if that particular rune was engraved on it. However, the process and types of runes used for this magic are unknown.

Besides your regular runes, there are also bind runes. Bind runes are ligatures that are made up of two or more runes. Historically, bind runes were mainly ornamental. In modern-day Paganism, bind runes are used to refer to a magical system of sigilization. Its creation involves building a monogram out of runes that have a meaning that is complementary to the bindrune's intended purpose. They look similar to the practice of Galdrastafir, but their processes are vastly different and require initiation and guidance to learn.

Runes are a tool that is used to guide the subconscious to focus on questions that are underlying one's mind. Some believe that the answers are provided by the subconscious, while others believe that the answer is sent by the divine to clarify that which we already know inside our hearts. Tacitus stated that runes are to be made from wood from any nut-bearing tree, including hazel, oak, pine, and cedar. It was popular to stain them red which is to symbolize blood.

The etymology of the word 'rune' is unknown, but it can only be found in the languages of the Germanic and Celtic people. This means that the word 'rune' is an ancient indigenous term. It was used to refer to things that were secret, secret laws, wisdom, and magical signs. Runes did not always refer to a single letter or word, instead, they could also refer to an abstract concept.

Runes were used alongside the present-day alphabet until the fourteenth century. In the first century AD, the Romans influenced most of Western Europe. The earliest runic inscriptions date back to 150 AD and were common in what is now known as Denmark, Northern Germany, and Southern Sweden. The oldest runes were found on coins, suit buckles, weapons, and implements. They were often the names of the owner or the person who made the item.

Runic stones were erected in the Viking Age to commemorate powerful leaders and heroic achievements. Shorter inscriptions could be found on everyday artifacts in Viking towns and markets. Vikings carved runes into stone, wood, or iron. As these materials were hard, runes had an angular shape.

Runes are phonetic symbols. In the Viking Age, runes were only used by people living in the Nordic area. Vikings traveled the world, bringing their runes and runic inscriptions with them. Runic inscriptions can be found in England, Greece, Russia, Turkey, and Greenland.

## *The Legend of the Runes*

There is much debate regarding the historical beginnings of runic writing, but there is a popular agreement on an outline of where they come from. Scholars presume that runes were sourced from one of the Old Italic alphabets that were used among the people of the Mediterranean in the first century, CE. These people inhabited the southern Germanic tribes. Early Germanic sacred symbols have been stored in Northern European petroglyphs. These petroglyphs are thought to have also inspired the creation of the runic alphabet.

The Norse Pagans believed that Odin was responsible for humans having access to the runic alphabet. When Odin hung from the branches of Yggdrasil for nine days and nine nights, it is said that he was gifted with the runes on the ninth night. There are no records of the runes written on paper. Many runes were carved into runestones that are now scattered across Northern Europe. The runic alphabet changes over the centuries and branches off into four known alphabets.

## The Elder Futhark (c. 160-700 CE)

The first of the runic alphabets, Elder Futhark, was an old Germanic runic alphabet that contained two dozen symbols. The first six symbols spell out the word "Futhark". The name of the alphabet is derived from these first six letters. As the Norse people began to move around Europe, the form and meanings of the runes changed to adapt to their new lifestyles and social structures, forming a new alphabet.

The Elder Futhark consists of 24 runes. These runes were scattered across all the Germanic cultures during the Scandinavian Iron Age. These runic symbols were written as a rune row and divided into three-eighths or ætts. There were eight runes in each ætt. The first ætt was known as Frey's ætt, the second as Hagal's ætt, and the third as Tyr's ætt.

Germanic runes had the same meaning as

Scandinavian runes, but their meanings began to change in the different Proto-Germanic and Proto-Norse languages. Their names and sounds began to differ slightly, and three more runes were added.

## The Younger Futhark (c. 700 - c. 1200 CE)

The Younger Futhark is also known as the Scandinavian alphabet. It originates from the Viking Age and was a simplified version of the Germanic Elder Futhark runes. It had 16 characters instead of 19, tailored for the Old Norse language. Each rune is a letter in the Old Norse alphabet, and they each represent a sound. Each rune carries a name that can be construed as the meaning associated with the rune, but not every rune carries much meaning on top of the sound that it creates. The Younger Futhark is divided into two different styles that are dependent on where the person was living at the time. Longer, branch-like runes were common in Denmark, while shorter, twig-like runes were common in Sweden and Norway. When runes were written upside down, their meaning would be opposite to their original meaning.

## *Anglo-Saxon/ Anglo-Frisian Futhorc (c. 5th century - c. 1,000 CE)*

Derived from the Elder Futhark, this runic alphabet was added from four and eight extra runes. This alphabet was a method to scribe Old English and Old Frisian. Old Frisian would not use the last two runes of the rune row that were added to write Old English. There are fewer than two hundred inscriptions of runes from this particular alphabet. They were mainly written on personal items, stone crosses, crosses, coins, and weapons. This runic alphabet held strong against Christianization until the end of the tenth century CE.

## *Medieval Futhork (Fully Formed in c. thirteenth century CE)*

In Scandinavia, around the late 10th century CE and c. 1200 CE, the Younger Futhark gradually changed to the Medieval Futhork. Its form remained consistent by the thirteenth century CE. This version of the runic alphabet stuck mainly to the 16 Younger Futhark runes. However, a few additions were added to the runes, such as dots to set apart specific sound values. These runes were not counted as separate runes, instead, they were recognized as the undotted version of the same rune. By the thirteenth century CE, Medieval Futhork began to double some of the consonant runes. This began to increase the use of bind runes. Runes remained a companion to the Roman alphabet during the Middle Ages. They were also used in personal letters, merchants' labels, manuscripts, and amulets.

## Rune Divination

Modern-day rune divination uses the same methods of divination that were used by the Norse Pagans. You can use this form of divination to connect to your higher self, gain inner guidance, offer advice, and tap into your intuition. Rune Divination uses the three sets of the Elder Futhark to interpret the runes. They tell the story of the life cycle. The first set of runes represents the more physical aspects of life, which include your material possessions and finding your path in life. The second set is used to interpret how you have matured and grown. It includes rune interpretations that pertain to obstacles that you will encounter, your fate, and the type of harvest you can expect. The third set of runes is used to interpret how you have developed spiritually, and what your legacy looks like in terms of your birth, community, intuition, and inheritance.

Traditionally, rune divination casts the runes in

multiples of three because the number three is a number of magical significance in Norse Paganism. The runes would be thrown (cast) onto a special piece of fabric while the caster looked up to the heavens. The runes that landed upright would be read and interpreted. The second method involved holding the pouch of runes with your non-dominant hand and thinking about the question that you want to be answered as you pull the runes out with your dominant hand, placing them in a specific sequence. Each rune in the sequence would be representative of a specific aspect of your life.

There are typically three types of rune layouts. A simple layout for beginners is the cross layout. The bottom rune of the cross-shape represents the basic influences that would impact the question. The rune on the left of the layout would indicate the possible problems that could influence the question. The top rune indicates the positives that may influence the question.

The rune on the right shows the immediate answer to the question. The rune in the middle of the cross demonstrated the future influences that could affect your question. If you decide to work on rune divination, then you can begin with the cross layout before progressing to harder styles of layout that will give you in-depth answers about your life in terms of personal matters, relationships, money, and business matters.

## Tarot

Tarot is a tool that can be used to tap into your intuition. It is not the act of fortune telling that is popular in the movies. Tarot has been used to provide guidance and answer questions for many years. Originating in Italy in the 1440s, tarot was first used as a parlor game before people began to use them for contacting the spirit world. The tarot deck is made up of 78 cards. 22 of the cards are called the "major arcana". The major arcana deal with the bigger events in your life. The remaining 56 cards are called the "minor arcana". They represent the smaller, but no less important, aspects of your life.

Each card is representative of something, but it is interpreted in the context of the card's position in the layout, your question, and the circumstances of the question. Tarot is a personal and customizable practice that can be used to strengthen your intuition and gain insight into events in your life.

**Doing a Tarot Reading**
The tarot deck is held in one hand. The practitioner will take a deep breath to center themselves and think about the question that they want to be answered. This allows them to meditate on their question until they are ready to shuffle the cards. Before shuffling, the

practitioner will knock on the cards to distribute their energy. Then they will shuffle. After thoroughly shuffling the cards, they will be set back into a single deck. Now the practitioner is ready to begin pulling out cards while they also think of their question.

A pause is taken after removing each card. The card that has been removed will be placed on the cloth or table in the shape of the layout that you have chosen. Each card will be examined so that the practitioner can first derive their own meaning from the card before they look up the card's actual meaning so that they can interpret the question in terms of its context. The tarot deck should be cleansed after each session using methods such as crystals, incense, essential oils, herbs, smoke wands, or white light visualization.

In terms of card layouts, like with rune

divination, you can begin with the simpler layouts before progressing to the harder layouts that will require more work but provide you with an in-depth answer about multiple aspects of your life. A classic beginner layout is the one-card pull. This method allows you to answer a yes or no question by interpreting the card using your intuition and by studying the meaning of the card in the context of the question that you asked. From there, you can progress to a three-card pull, which will give you an answer to your question in terms of your past, present, and future, and then on to harder, more in-depth layouts.

## Astrology

You may be familiar with Greco-Roman astrology, which is the most common form of astrology used in the modern-day. However, Norse Paganism also utilizes astrology to gain spiritual and psychological insights. This type of astrology is especially accurate for those of Northern and Central European descent.

In general, astrology is based on the notion that celestial bodies hold a specific influence over us, just as the moon influences the tides. We can choose to tune into this subtle cosmic energy while still having the free will to make our own choices and decisions that will influence our futures. Astrology provides you with a guide to determine how you want to move forward and live your life.

Western astrology is based on an ancient Babylonian practice that studies celestial bodies (and planets) by observing what energy is dominant, and what that means on a specific day, as a result of the celestial body's position in the sky. Zodiac signs were created based on what constellation was behind the sun on the day you were born. This process developed further to include the elements of fire, earth, air, and water. In turn, this began to inspire the inclusion of other characteristics and traits in the interpretation of your zodiac sign. The moon moves through a zodiac sign every 2.5 days, as well as a specific zodiac season.

**Planets**

In Norse astrology, there is a balance between men and women. They use the Norse pantheon of gods and goddesses to describing planetary energy. The most important planets are the following:

- Odin represents the moon.
- Freya represents the sun.

The female planetary energy manifests with Mercury who represents Skadhi, and the following planets representing the Norse goddesses:

- Venus represents Frigga.
- Neptune represented the Norn goddesses.

The male planetary energy manifests with Mars representing Thor, and the following planets representing the Norse gods:

- Jupiter represents Freyr.
- Saturn represents Tyr.
- Uranus represents Loki. Loki has also been found to assume the feminine form as a result of his shape-shifting abilities.

As the moon takes on a North declination, it will represent Heimdall. When the moon takes on a Southern declination, it represents Hel. In Norse astrology, the planets have a stronger affinity with the houses than they do with the zodiac signs, which are also known as runes in Norse astrology. The gender balance of the planetary energies provides a clearer meaning of the houses and archetypal runes.

## Houses

There are eight solar houses of ancient heathen and pagan tradition. The meaning and placement of the house are easily understood and clear. The eternal dimensions of day versus night, and self versus other, define how the houses function within your natal (birth) horoscope. The following houses are represented in conjunction with certain Norse gods and goddesses:

- Night-West house is associated with the Norns.

- The Night house is associated with Skadhi.

- The Night-East house is associated with Frigga.

- The East house is associated with Freyja.

- The Day-East house is associated with Thor.

- The Day house is associated with Freyr.

- The Day-West house is associated with Tyr.

- The West house is associated with Loki.

- Odin is not associated with any house as he is considered an eternal wanderer.

## Runes

The planet's position along the ecliptic is defined by 24 equal-sized runes. Runes are used to describe the twenty-first-century cosmic forces that influence our lives. They provide a universal archetype that can be used to explain our attributes, as well as those of the world. Runes are independent of the millennial drift of constellations, meaning that they are essentially eternal.

# CHAPTER 11
# NORSE PAGAN PATHWAYS

Norse Paganism has changed over the centuries as Norse communities evolved. Through trade and migration, the Norse people met new people with different religions and belief systems. They would sometimes integrate the beliefs of these communities if it suited how they lived their lives. This resulted in subtle changes in Norse Paganism between communities as the years went by. These subtle changes formed what is referred to as pathways, which are different forms of Norse Paganism but they have a similar origin.

## The Different Pathways

The reawakening of Norse Paganism in the present has also experienced similar changes and additions to the religion. Norse Paganism in the present is very similar to the original Norse Paganism practiced by the ancient Norse people. However, modern-day life means we now live in conjunction with technology, as well as certain laws that result in some practices, such as blood sacrifices, being made illegal. The appropriate changes have been made to these practices, allowing the religion to adapt. This adaptation resulted in a new form of Norse Paganism forming.

This new form is a branch of the original version of Norse Paganism. There are multiple branches, called pathways, that have developed since the late nineteenth century. These Norse Pagan pathways allow individuals in the present to follow Norse Paganism in a manner that is suited to their lifestyles and what they are comfortable believing in. Often, the pathway speaks to the person and feels like the right decision for them. Below is a brief introduction to the common pathways that are followed today.

## *Vanatru*

This pathway celebrates and worships the Vanir gods. The name Vanatru means "true to the Vanir". It emerged in the late 90s as an alternative Norse Pagan pathway, Ásatrú. This pathway is focused on witchcraft, folk magic, divination, and nature as the Vanir gods and goddesses were gods of fertility, the life cycle, and magic. This pathway is a solitary pathway. It treats the gods as individuals with their own specific rites and communication methods. It has less structure than Ásatrú.

## *Rökkatru*

Coined by Abby Hellasdottir, this term means "true to the Rökkr". The Rökkr are dark entities such as the Jötunn and giants of Norse mythology. They represent death, chaos, and the primordial elements, such as the fire and ice that were used to create the world. In Norse Paganism, darkness and chaos are not considered evil. They are accepted as a necessary part of our lives and the life cycle. It is as important to understand this pathway and its deities as it is to worship the Aesir and Vanir. Typically, this pathway is linked to Norse shamanism.

## *Thursatru*

A pre-Christian belief and sorcerous practice that focuses on the worship of the Thurses— antagonistic giants found in the underworld and beyond. This practice focuses on tapping into energy called the "Current", by using tools such as invocations and bind runes. Practitioners believe that our essence originates from a place found beyond the cosmos. They have a belief in chaos originating from the Ginnungagap. The Aesir and the Jötunn are considered to be enemies of the followers of this pathway.

## **Lokean**

This pathway is a personal practice that focuses its worship on Loki as a primary deity. Loki is a god of chance who is aligned with happy accidents. Loki teaches his followers lessons so that they learn self-respect and how to live in accordance with their chosen destiny. His mischievous behavior allows him to enforce a balance between order and chaos, instigating action by others. His honor code is flexible, allowing him to adapt and transform so that he can continuously work to better himself and be authentic to who he is. This is something that his followers aim to embody. Followers of this pathway learn that nothing is permanent, except for change.

## *Odinism*

Odinism has nothing to do with the worship of Odin. This pathway is a race-based, Folkish Norse Pagan movement that originates from the Germanic Völkisch Movement. It is a racialist movement that has nothing to do with any of the other Norse Pagan pathways. It was an element that was essential to the Folkish beliefs that ended in Nazism. It became the first form of Heathenry in the United States of America, though Heathenism cannot be used as a synonym for Odinism as they have vastly different beliefs and values. However, this is part of why Norse Paganism and Viking imagery and beliefs have a negative and racist image in the modern world.

## *Heathenry*

Heathenism is a modern neo-pagan spirituality that is informed by the folklore, customs, beliefs, and worldviews of pre-Christian Northern European civilizations. Practitioners of this pathway are called "Heathens". The following points are the central ideas of Heathenry.

### It Is a Decentralized Religion

This means that Heathenry has no core ideology. There are no holy books, scriptures, or key religious figures. The *Poetic Edda* and the *Prose Edda* are not considered religious texts, even though they contain information pertaining to Norse Paganism. This pathway lacks the high demand for worship that other religions, such as Christianity, require. This is also why modern Heathenry varies depending on the person, the group of people, and where they live.

**Animistic**

We have already discussed animism in Chapter 2. Animism applies here too because Heathens believe that everything is interconnected simply because it exists. When you interact with your world, you form connections with its spirits, energy, and magic of your own accord. These relationships create a sense of connection. Ceremonial components allow you to participate in this natural world. This connection looks different for everyone, as they do not state that there is a correct connection to divinity.

**Pluralistic**

This means that Heathenry believes that everything contains multitudes. Every aspect of the world and life is built on numerous principles. These principles have truths that constantly change. Heathenism doesn't view people as forces of good or evil, and there is no principal force that controls every aspect of the world and life.

## Polytheistic

Heathens believe in multiple gods and goddesses. Their gods include the Norse gods, and some Heathens may include the gods of other religions. No god is central in Norse Paganism as a whole. The gods all have varying levels of popularity. The decision to worship a specific god or goddess is up to the individual and their needs.

## Immanent

Heathenry focuses on the quality, actualization, and fulfillment of our current lives and the relationships that we have with the world around us. These practices and observances are centered on our immediate reality, well-being, and lived experience. Norse Heathenry focuses on experienced animism and the relationships that we cultivate with ourselves and others.

## Orthopraxic

A core approach of Heathenism is valuing their life experiences, the integrity of their practices and behavior, and the creation of their legacy. Essentially, it focuses on what is right for that person.

## *Ásatrú*

This religious movement is the most popular form of Norse Paganism that is practiced in the modern world. This religious movement is the pathway closest to the original version of Norse Paganism. It was started in the nineteenth century and was first recognized as an official religion in Iceland, in 1973. The name Ásatrú means "true to the Aesir gods". It is a community-based religion–meaning individuals act for the benefit of the group.

Individual Ásatrú organizations are called "kindred". Their priests are called "Gothar" and their priestesses are known as "Gythia". A congregation is known as 'Folk". The main guidelines of this pathway are based on the information that is found in the *Hávamál*. The offerings and ceremonies of this pathway are similar to the original offerings and ceremonies of Norse Paganism.

In recent years, Norse Paganism has re-emerged as a religion. In the twenty-first century, Norse Paganism has a small but devoted group of followers who are mainly found in Scandinavia and North America. This ancient religion is known for being remembered and becoming mythology even after the number of followers dwindled with the introduction of Christianity. It has gained even more popularity as movie corporations have decided to gain inspiration for their newer movies and comic books from Norse mythology.

However, this portrayal has led to its own issues. Radical groups have seen these masculine, tough images of superheroes associated with Norse Paganism and decided to adopt Norse Pagan elements and interpret them in a way that suits their needs. This does not mean that their belief in Norse Paganism is an accurate representation of the religion. If anything, it's the opposite. Norse Paganism has never taught that the races of people make them inherently unequal. Many elements, images, and Norse Pagan beliefs have been hijacked for the self-serving purposes of certain groups.

One notable, and easily recognized, a symbol that has been stolen by white supremacists is Thor's hammer. This symbol has been adopted as a symbol of power and masculinity by this group. They aim to use this symbol to convince others that they are superior because of their race. However, this symbol is not one of power, it is a way for the Norse Pagans to connect with their gods, just as the traditional cross is a way for the Christians to connect with their god.

In this section, we will discuss the true history of Ásatrú, its beliefs, festivals, gods and goddesses, structure, and magic.

## The History of Ásatrú

The history of Asatru is the history of Norse Paganism. The establishment of Norse Paganism is not a part of recorded history as the Norse people were an oral culture. Germanic Paganism began to decline at the end of the Viking Age because it was not Evangelistic and the Roman Catholic Church was determined to evangelize the inhabitants of Scandinavia. Their efforts were well-funded and supported by those in powerful positions in society.

Ásatrú is a revived form of Norse Paganism originating in twentieth-century Iceland. Sveinbjörn Beinteinsson, an Icelandic farmer, founded the modern Ásatrú faith. Ásatrú is commonly found in Scandinavia and North America. He sought to revive the old Scandinavian belief system by recruiting followers and writing poetry.

Beginning in the 1970s, this revival of Germanic Paganism began on the summer solstice. It was recognized as an official religion in 1973, and its full name is Íslenska Ásatrúarfélagið. In the United States, another group of this same religion became known as the Asatru Free Assembly, which then became the Asatru Folk Assembly. Many Norse Pagans who follow the Ásatrú pathway prefer to be called "heathens" over terms such as "neo-pagan". Either way, this pathway is very similar in its modern form to its form before the Christianisation of Norse cultures. In the present, many Ásatrú and

Heathen groups are publicly denouncing white supremacists who have co-opted the symbols of the Norse Pagans to further their racist agenda.

**Beliefs**

As we have already discussed, the followers of this pathway believe in the Aesir gods, however, some followers do include gods and goddesses from the Vanir or other religions. Either way, they believe that the gods are living beings who take active roles in the world and interact with its inhabitants. *The Nine Noble Virtues of Ásatrú* in Chapter 2 are also applied here. These virtues may be named specifically for Ásatrú, but they are derived from the original virtues and values of Norse Paganism. They value people who work hard. They believe that as a person you have the right to happiness, strength, a strong community, friends, and security. You must be loyal, hospitable, courageous, and wise, as they are the main goals of this path. They believe in celebrating your ancestors as they are always with you, even in death. They also believe in the afterlife. You need to be loyal to your family, whether they are family by blood or sworn members of the family. The gods must be honored through offerings. These offerings usually involve offering environmentally safe objects that can decompose; such as food or wooden items. The governing of a community should be a group effort of the entire community. They do not believe in hiding who you are.

**The Structure of Ásatrú**

The Ásatrú community is divided into separate groups called "Kindreds" which are your local worship groups. Members may be related through blood or marriage. The Kindred are led by a Goðar, who is a priest (or chieftain) who is responsible for speaking for the gods and goddesses.

## Gods and Goddesses

The main Norse deities worshiped by the followers of this path are the Aesir gods. Their main gods and goddesses include Odin, Thor, Freyr, Loki, Freya, and Frigg.

## Ásatrú Magic

This pathway of Norse Paganism is mainly spiritual in origin. However, many modern-day Pagans will follow the teachings of seiðr magic. The use of runes for divination is also quite common for Norse Pagans who practice magic in the modern world.

## Festivals and Ceremonies

The modern-day ceremonies of Ásatrú have been modified so that they are suitable for modern sensibilities. This ensures that no one does anything illegal or accidentally cruel. These ceremonies mainly involve eating and drinking rituals that symbolize the beliefs of the community. Sacrifices have been modified to use non-living objects such as food, drink, and biodegradable objects that are made out of environmentally friendly materials. The festivals celebrated by the Ásatrú community are very similar to the original Norse Pagan festivals, however, their names and/or their dates have changed slightly to accommodate modern life, but what the festivals celebrate has remained the same with minor adaptations. These festivals include:

- Disfest: January 31
- Ostara: March 21
- Walpurgis: April 30
- Midsummer Blot: June 21
- Freysblot: August 1
- Harvestfest: September 21
- Winternights: October 31
- Yule: January 1

One festival that has no set date is known as Sumbel. Sumbel is a formalized religious toasting ceremony that is held whenever the community needs to hold it. A ceremonial horn, filled with either mead or ale, is passed around by those in attendance. Each participant will make either a toast, boast about success, or say something significant over the horn before taking a drink. It is important that whatever is said is thoughtful and meaningful.

# CHAPTER 12
# NORSE PAGANISM IN THE MODERN WORLD

The survival of Norse Paganism through its mythology has allowed for a revival of this ancient religion. This revival has mainly taken on the form of the Norse Pagan pathways of Heathenism and Ásatrú. This belief system was able to withstand the introduction of Christianity to Northern Europe, which wiped out many ancient religions. However, the shape of this religion changed with this introduction and the number of Norse Pagans began to decline after the Viking Age. While it may not have survived all these years as an active religion, it is still well-known for its continued endurance.

In recent years, we have seen the interpretation and understanding of Norse Paganism change as it moved away from being solely mythology. It started to gain ground as a religion in the form of pathways, the most popular and common versions being Ásatrú and Heathenism. Unfortunately, this increase in popularity came in the form of the media using Norse mythology as inspiration for new media properties that do not always positively, or accurately, display the Norse people and their religion.

This has created assumptions about what Norse Paganism is, and the type of people who follow these religious paths. People began adopting Norse imagery and twisting its meanings to suit their agendas, even when Norse Paganism does not teach their ideals. White supremacist groups in the United States have co-opted Norse images to further their racist agenda, even though Norse Paganism does not teach that any race is unequal to another. Unfortunately, this is only one of the many misconceptions about Norse Paganism.

## Norse Pagan Misconceptions

### *In The Media*

With the arrival of the popular Thor movies, many of the fans began to take an interest in Norse mythology. Fans of Loki and Thor in particular contributed to this popularity, and unfortunately, it wasn't only because of the beauty of the characters. The powerful image of Thor with his hammer and unstoppable power appealed to many men, but unfortunately, it also appealed to groups that wished to co-opt this symbol of power and status.

The impact of the media on Norse Paganism has left the knowledge of the gods either severely lacking or completely inaccurate. Thor is portrayed only as the god of thunder in many comic books and movies. In Norse Paganism, Thor has a variety of roles that he plays. Although Thor is named the god of thunder, this symbolizes his ability to take control and influence the weather. This ability is what caused him to be recognized as a type of weather god in the agricultural Norse communities. These communities believed that at the end of the winter, Thor would battle the frost giants, who represented destructive natural forces, so that spring could arrive. They made offerings to Thor when they needed the rain to water their crops.

The media portrays Loki as a misunderstood god who had a rough childhood and is now taking his frustrations out on humanity. This is an inaccurate depiction of who Loki is as a Norse god. The Lokean pathway has described Loki as not only the god of mischief, but also as an enforcer of the balance between chaos and order. In the Eddic poems, he challenges the other gods when their norms are being broken, such as when Odin decided to study seiðr magic. Loki mocked him because this form of magic is seen as a feminine act. Loki instigates a person to take any action that allows them to remain true to themselves and be authentic. In this case, Odin carried on studying seiðr magic and became extremely proficient in it. He was true to himself in doing so, as Odin is always working to gain more knowledge. This demonstrates one of the instances whereby Loki aims to encourage a person to remain true to who they are, even if others do not approve.

### *Hate Groups*

The Norse people were made up of various races

and ethnicities, as supported by the DNA analysis of skeletons dating to the Viking Age. The Norse people traveled so that they could trade with other communities and settle in new areas. When they decided to settle in a new environment, they would often adapt to the culture and religion that was originally there. Settling in new areas also meant that they would intermarry with members of the indigenous communities.

This debunked the theory of the Nazis that stated that the Norse people were, what they considered to be, a pure race upon which they built their ideals. White supremacists have adopted this false idea. In reality, the Norse people were able to peacefully coexist and trade with the people along with the Canadian to Afghanistan trade routes, this included the ancestors of the Inuits and Sámi peoples. They were able to embrace a variety of cultures into their own so that they could continue living peacefully, allowing their communities to flourish alongside their new friends.

## The Revival of Norse Paganism

This book has already discussed many of the aspects of this ancient religion of the Nordic people. Many inaccuracies and negative connotations exist in the present, however, the information is available to see that Norse Paganism is about living in harmony with your world. Norse Pagnism's newfound popularity is not all bad. With it came the opportunity to further the study of the Norse people, whose oral culture meant that we have very little written historical information on the lives they led.

The study of Norse Paganism shows that there is no foundation to support the belief of radical groups, the belief that there should be a separation between the communities and that people should be unequally treated. The Norse Pagan belief of animism is one of the points that demonstrates how the Norse people valued everyone they came into contact with, and embraced what they learned from their interactions with new cultures. Their incorporation of these new, foreign elements into their beliefs to create an ever-changing religion demonstrates their tolerance and respect for other people, no matter who they were.

The revival of Norse Paganism in the 1970s saw the Norse Pagan pathway, Ásatrú gaining ground as a modern-day version of Norse Paganism. This pathway has been adapted to fit the rules and technological developments of the twenty-first century. While it has few followers, they still believe that Norse Paganism is a way of life meant to ensure the flourishing of their community and doing what needs to be done for the benefit of others. They act in accordance with the *Nine Noble Virtues of Ásatrú*. One of their core beliefs is that you do not wield power over others, and you do not use any power that you *do* have to hurt others.

Many misconceptions exist in modern-day society, but the truth behind Norse Paganism will always be there. It is not only a religion, but also a way of life that is meant to help you lead a fulfilling existence, one which is in harmony with your environment. It also ensures that you remain authentic to the person that you are. Misconceptions will, unfortunately, always exist, but so will the truth. As modern-day Norse Paganism adapts and changes with technological (and societal) developments, its core beliefs and values will remain constant. It will be an ever-present foundation that allows anyone who follows this pathway to create a version of Norse Paganism that is true to who they are.

# CONCLUSION

Norse Paganism is more than a religion, it is a way of life. From the ancient Norse people to modern-day Norse Pagans, the roots of Norse Paganism have buried themselves deep into our society. While the phrases "Norse Pagan" and "Norse mythology" are used interchangeably, this old religion has survived the centuries, the rise and fall of empires, and the introduction of new, more popular religions. It is able to adapt and overcome challenges while remaining true to its core elements. Even the misappropriation of

Norse Pagan symbols and images has not been enough to finally put an end to it. It has, and will continue, to thrive, so long as we pass down the knowledge, beliefs, and values of this way of life to our children and theirs.

## What did we cover?

Chapter 1 created the foundation of the book. To understand why Norse Paganism has been able to survive all these years, we needed to understand who the Norse people were and how their communities began to change over time. By understanding that the Norse people were mainly agricultural communities, you begin to understand their reasoning behind wanting to branch off and move to new areas in Northern Europe. This branching off allowed them to introduce new, foreign elements to their version of Norse Paganism, so that their belief system would be better adapted to their way of life.

The oral culture of the Norse Pagans means that we do not have much recorded information on how they lived. Scholars have to rely on archeological evidence and the few surviving Norse literary texts, as well as the spoken information that has been passed down over the centuries. However, one solid piece of information that scholars have been able to agree on is that Norse Paganism today looks very similar to the Norse Paganism of the ancient Norse people. It is one of the few surviving religions that can boast such a fact.

In Chapter 2, the values and beliefs of the Norse Pagans were discussed. As Norse Paganism has changed over time to better suit the current way of life, we focused on the core elements and ideas of these beliefs and values. These core elements were compiled using information obtained from scholars and Norse literary texts, such as the Eddas. The fact that Norse Paganism today is very similar to the Norse Paganism of old means that we were also able to study the virtues of the modern Norse Pagan pathway Ásatrú to gain a more detailed insight into their values. Some of the more important elements of Norse Pagan beliefs included that they were a polytheistic culture that welcomed their interactions with people from other religions because they felt comfortable welcoming their gods into the Norse pantheon. The Norse Pagans were very respectful of humans, animals, and inanimate objects because they believed that everything was connected.

Their belief in fate showed that the Norse Pagans did not believe in simply resigning yourself to your fate. Instead, you should confront it, and fight back with honor so that you can still lead the life you want to live, even though you cannot deceive or change your fate. These beliefs demonstrated the type of people the ancient Norse Pagans were. In the present, these beliefs show the type of people that Norse

Pagans are striving to become.

Their values are known as the *Nine Noble Virtues of Ásatrú*. While Ásatrú is a modern-day Norse Pagan pathway, it is the pathway that is the closest to the original practices and structure of Norse Paganism that was practiced by the ancient Norse people. These virtues were based on the information found in Norse texts, including the *Hávamál*, the *Poetic Edda,* and the *Prose Edda*, as well as the Icelandic sagas. These values include elements such as having the courage to stand up for what's right—even when others do not—and to persevere even when you make mistakes or face defeat. This chapter teaches you that while Norse Paganism is a way of life; you still have to play an active role in your life.

The spiritual practices of the Norse Pagans were covered in Chapter 3. Through a brief look at a radical version of Norse Paganism known as "the way of fire and ice", we were able to discuss Norse Paganism in terms of it being a living tradition. This tradition is intended to serve the community, while teaching you to live in a way that is authentic to who you are. It also emphasized the importance of not using your power to abuse or be used against others.

Their spiritual practices included things such as sacrifices—known as *blót*—that mainly involved the killing of animals. In times of famine and war, human sacrifice would occur only once their community had carefully thought of the reasons and intentions behind this practice. The deposition of items, such as food, drink, jewelry, and weapons, was used to honor the gods that they worshiped in the hopes of receiving their blessing.

Rites of passage were used to welcome both

newborn and adopted children into a family—accompanied by a specific ritual—and marriage and burial rites. Their sacred spaces were mainly found in nature. These spaces could take the form of an open-air altar or a stone altar. The ancient Norse Pagans did make use of temples that were dedicated to a specific god depending on where they lived. Their festivals and ceremonies were used to celebrate their spiritual practices. These celebrations have changed slightly in name and date over the years, but the essence of these festivals has remained the same. They were mainly based on the agricultural nature of the communities. This means that their celebrations usually celebrated things such as the harvest and planting seasons.

Chapter 4 discussed the most important Norse literary texts that have been preserved and studied over the years. These texts include the *Poetic Edda* and the *Prose Edda*, as well as the Icelandic sagas. The most well-known author of the Eddas was Snorri Sturluson. Sturluson was a poet, scholar, and historian of the Norse people. He compiled the *Prose Edda* by using the information contained in the *Poetic Edda*, whose author is unknown. The Eddas mainly consisted of poetry; the Icelandic sagas, such as the *Volsunga Saga* and the *Laxdaela Saga*, consisted of stories and songs written about the Norse gods, popular heroes, and heroines, past Norse kings, and their ancestors. These poems and stories provide modern-day scholars with insight into how the Norse people lived and what their belief system looked like. They are the main credible sources of information available about the Norse people in the present, however, some translations of the work are influenced by the Christianization of Scandinavia.

Chapter 5 studied the Norse Pagan creation myth. The Norse Pagans believed that before life of any kind existed, the world had only a realm of fire and a realm of ice that surrounded an empty void, known as the Ginnungagap. The meeting of these two elements in the Ginnungagap created the sparks needed for the first life forms, Ymir and Audhumbla, to be created. Their creation began a chain of events that would lead to the creation of the gods and goddesses, the death of the frost giants, and the creation of the world. It is important to understand the creation myth, as many of the beliefs of the Norse Pagans are rooted in their belief of how the world came into being. One of these beliefs is their belief in reincarnation.

The type of environments and beings that made up the nine realms was discussed in Chapter 6. While the description of the nine realms is not exceptionally detailed, it does give us an idea of what the Norse Pagans thought these realms looked like. This created the foundation for their beliefs in the magical creatures and beings that lived in these realms. An introduction to the nine realms provides a foundation for the magic and stories that resulted from their belief in the different realms and the creatures that lived there. This introduction is useful in helping us understand how the world is separated into the different realms, and how their inhabitants interact with each other.

Chapter 7 covered multiple topics, such as the types of gods and goddesses in Norse Paganism, and the creatures and beings that they believed in. We learned that there were originally two pantheons of gods who fought a war before they became the Norse pantheon that we are familiar with today. This chapter also covered the main gods that were worshiped in each pantheon. The creatures and beings in Norse Paganism are vast, however, we discussed those creatures and beings that frequently appeared in Norse mythology as they played an important role in their beliefs and legends. We discussed what they looked like, which realms they lived in, and why they were malevolent or benevolent, as well as their role in Norse Pagan beliefs.

In Chapter 8, we studied Ragnarök and its importance in the inevitable end and rebirth of the world. Essentially, it was the Norse Pagan version of the apocalypse. The signs of Ragnarök's arrival would start small before the signs would increase in intensity. These signs would lead to a battle between the gods and the giants. The key role-players in this battle were looked at to see that not even the gods were infallible. The devastation of the battle means that no clear winner or loser is indicated in the story. However, the creation myth discusses how the end of the world, the gods, and many other beings create the opportunity to start new. The Norse Pagan belief that everything will end before it can be reborn is rooted here. The surviving gods and goddesses will go on to create a new pantheon while learning from the mistakes of their predecessors. Humanity would be reborn from the two surviving humans who had hidden from the battle in the forest; this would parallel humanity's creation from the trees. Ragnarök teaches us that everything will eventually end, but it allows for the rebirth of something even better.

Chapter 9 moves away from the more fundamental concepts of Norse Paganism to discuss aspects that are not practiced by every Norse Pagan. Magic is not inherent to being a Norse Pagan. Yes, as a Norse Pagan you would believe in magic, but becoming a magic practitioner is different. It is a lifelong journey that does not suit every person who decides to become a Norse Pagan. Those who do decide to pursue a magical journey will usually choose to partake in seiðr magic. This form of magic focuses on developing your intuition and opening your mind by using divination techniques, trancework, and any other appropriate spiritual work.

From here we moved on to Chapter 10, which covered the tools that can be used to assist you on your journey of pursuing magic. These tools included runes, tarot, and astrology. While they mainly focused on divination, predicting the future is not their main purpose. These tools provide guidance by helping you answer questions and determine what outside influences may affect the answer you get. This chapter mainly focused on providing an introduction to these tools and how to use them so that you can make an informed decision on whether they are in line with the path of Norse Paganism that you want to follow.

Chapter 11 introduces us to the various Norse Pagan pathways that have developed over the years. In this chapter, we discussed how Heathenism and Ásatrú are the most common pathways, as their practices and beliefs are nearly identical to the Norse Paganism practiced by the ancient Norse people. The pathway that you decide to follow should be appropriate to the life you want to lead. You should also be comfortable with what this path entails. These pathways are a means of creating a modern-day community of Norse Pagans who can support each other and learn how to live a fulfilling life that respects the environment and your community.

Chapter 12 looked at Norse Paganism in the modern world. It covered a few of the misconceptions of Norse Paganism and how they affected its reputation. The revival of Norse Paganism was briefly discussed in this chapter as its revival mainly consisted of the pathway called Ásatrú, which had been discussed in detail in chapter 11. This chapter also reiterated that Ásatrú and Heathenism, as well as the other Norse Pagan pathways, have no connection with the racist and bigoted groups that are co-opting the Norse Pagan symbols and imagery to further their agenda. On a brighter note, this chapter briefly discussed how the increased popularity of the ancient Norse people has allowed for further continued study of their lives and their belief systems.

## Did We Deliver Our Promise?

*Norse Paganism for Beginners* has provided you with the information that you need to understand who the Norse people were, how their lives contributed to their beliefs as Norse Pagans, as well as discussing, in detail, various important aspects of the Norse Pagan belief system. While not all aspects of Norse Paganism could be given in great detail, we provided you with the necessary primer on each topic. By connecting the topics and their content to each other, we were able to demonstrate how Norse Paganism is not simply a belief system or mythology; instead, it is a way of life.

## What Will You Take Away From This Book?

After reading this book, you should understand who the Norse Pagan people were, in the past and the present. You should now be able to view media that portrays the Norse people with a critical eye; be able to determine the historical truth, compared to what has been slanted by a particular bias. Your understanding of the content of this book should also give you the ability to decide what Norse Pagan pathway suits your lifestyle and outlook on life.

# REFERENCES

Andersson, K. (2022, March 4). *Old Nordic Symbols: Norse Runes & Viking Ornaments (Meanings & Examples)*. Nordicperspective.com. https://nordicperspective.com/history/vikings/nordic-symbols-norse-runes

Andren, A. (2005). Behind "Heathendom": Archaeological Studies of Old Norse Religion. In *Jstor.org* (pp. 105–138). https://www.jstor.org/stable/27917543?seq=1

Centre of Excellence. (2018, October 29). *A Guide to Norse Gods and Goddesses*. Centre of Excellence. https://www.centreofexcellence.com/norse-gods-goddesses/

Crawford, J. (2018). *Basic Beliefs of Asatru*. Https://Corespirit.com; Core Spirit. https://corespirit.com/articles/basic-beliefs-asatru

Debutify. (2020, January 30). *Norse Mythology Creatures*. VikingsBrandTM. https://www.vikingsbrand.co/blogs/norse-news/norse-mythology-creatures

Eclectic Magick. (2016). *Asatru*. Eclectic-Magick.com. https://eclectic-magick.com/forecast/asatru/

Edred, T. (2013). *Runelore: The Magic, History, and Hidden Codes of the Runes*. Google Books. https://books.google.co.za/books?id=TL_lPRMWAdMC&printsec=frontcover#v=onepage&q&f=false

Franz Josef Stern. (2011). Norse Astrology, Norse Horoscopes - Superior to Traditional Greco-Roman Astrology? *EzineArticles*. https://ezinearticles.com/?Norse-Astrology,-Norse-Horoscopes---Superior-to-Traditional-Greco-Roman-Astrology?&id=6280132

Frater, J. (2018, August 6). *10 Interesting Viking Rituals*. Listverse.com. https://listverse.com/2018/08/06/10-interesting-viking-rituals/

Geller, P. (2016, October 20). *Aesir - Norse Gods*. Mythology.net. https://mythology.net/norse/norse-gods/aesir/

Gill, N. S. (2017). *How Did the Norse Believe the World Was Created?* Learn Religions. https://www.learnreligions.com/creation-in-norse-mythology-117868

Greenberg, M. (2020a, November 9). *The Norse

*Creation Myth*. MythologySource. https://mythologysource.com/norse-creation-myth/

Greenberg, M. (2020b, November 30). *The Nine Worlds of Norse Legend*. MythologySource. https://mythologysource.com/nine-worlds-norse/

Greenberg, M. (2021, February 16). *The Vanir Gods and Goddesses*. MythologySource. https://mythologysource.com/vanir-gods-and-goddesses/

Groeneveld, E. (2018). Runes. In *World History Encyclopedia*. World History Encyclopedia. https://www.worldhistory.org/runes/

Larsen, C. (2020, July 30). *What Did Norse Pagan Sacred Spaces and Altars Look Like?* Mage by Moonlight. https://magebymoonlight.com/norse-pagan-sacred-spaces-altars/

Lecouteux, C., & Moynihan, M. (2016). *Encyclopedia of Norse and Germanic folklore, mythology, and magic*. Inner Traditions.

Loptson, D. (2015, January 8). *What is a Lokean?* Polytheist.com. http://polytheist.com/orgrandr-lokean/2015/01/08/what-is-a-lokean/

Lori. (2017, December 9). T*he History of Yule and the Wild Hunt*.DIY Pagan.

https://diypagan.com/2017/12/08/the-history-of-yule-and-the-wild-hunt/#:~:text=It%20was%20a%20celebration%20during%20the%20Wild%20Hunt%2C,parties%20through%20the%20woods%20or%20across%20the%20sky.

Mandal, D. (2018, January 29). *The Most Powerful Norse Gods and Goddesses. Realm of History*. Realm of History. https://www.realmofhistory.com/2018/01/29/12-norse-gods-goddesses-facts/

Mark, J. J. (2018). Nine Realms of Norse Cosmology. In *World History Encyclopedia*. World History Encyclopedia. https://www.worldhistory.org/article/1305/nine-realms-of-norse-cosmology/

McKay, A. (2018, July 19). *Creatures in Norse Mythology*. Life in Norway. https://www.lifeinnorway.net/creatures-in-norse-mythology/

Mcmaster, G. (2021). *White supremacists are misappropriating Norse mythology, says expert*. Ualberta.ca. https://www.ualberta.ca/folio/2020/07/white-supremacists-are-misappropriating-norse-mythology-says-expert.html

Merriam-Webster. (n.d.-a). *Cremation*. Merriam-Webster.com. Retrieved April 14, 2022, from https://www.merriam-webster.com/dictionary/cremation

Merriam-Webster. (n.d.-b). *Germanic*. Merriam-Webster.com. Retrieved April 14, 2022, from https://www.merriam-webster.com/dictionary/Germanic

Merriam-Webster. (n.d.-c). *Inhume*. Merriam-Webster.com. Retrieved April 14, 2022, from https://www.merriam-webster.com/dictionary/inhumation

Merriam-Webster. (n.d.-d). *Ouroboros*. Merriam-Webster.com. Retrieved April 14, 2022, from https://www.merriam-webster.com/dictionary/Ouroboros

Merriam-Webster. (n.d.-e). *Pagan*. Merriam-Webster.com. Retrieved April 14, 2022, from https://www.merriam-webster.com/dictionary/pagan

Merriam-Webster. (n.d.-f). *Proto-Germanic*. Merriam-Webster.com. Retrieved April 14, 2022, from https://www.merriam-webster.com/dictionary/Proto-Germanic

Merriam-Webster. (n.d.-g). *Runes*. Merriam-Webster.com. Retrieved April 14, 2022, from https://www.merriam-webster.com/dictionary/runes

Merriam-Webster. (n.d.-h). *Skald*. Merriam-Webster.com. Retrieved April 14, 2022, from https://www.merriam-webster.com/dictionary/skaldic#other-words

Merriam-Webster. (n.d.-i). *Tarot*. Merriam-Webster.com. Retrieved April 14, 2022, from https://www.merriam-webster.com/dictionary/tarot

Merriam-Webster. (2022). *Norse*. Merriam-Webster.com. https://www.merriam-webster.com/dictionary/Norse

Milner, R. (2021, December 9). *Here's what Norse pagans believe today*. Grunge.com. https://www.grunge.com/701969/heres-what-norse-pagans-believe-today/

*Norse Holidays and Festivals*. (2022). Wizardrealm.com. http://wizardrealm.com/norse/holidays.html

Otherworldly Oracle. (2021, December 29). *Norse Magic: Seidr, Shapeshifting, Runes, & More*. https://otherworldlyoracle.com/norse-magic/

Planet Norway. (2021, August 11). *15 mythical Creatures from Norse mythology*. Planet Norway. https://planetnorway.com/norse-creatures/

Scandinavia Facts. (2020, March 30). *Is the Norse Religion Still Practiced Today?* Scandinavia Facts. https://scandinaviafacts.com/norse-religion-today/#:~:text=The%20Norse%20belief%20system%20is%20polytheistic%3B%20meaning%2C%20followers,Odin%20%E2%80%93%20Odin%20is%20the%20ruler%20of%20Valhalla.

Scandinavia Facts. (2021, March 9). *Can You Convert to the Norse Religion?* Scandinavia Facts. https://scandinaviafacts.com/convert-norse-religion/#:~:text=Although%20the%20nuances%20of%20modern%20Norse%20religion%20may,figure%20with%20numerous%20traits%2C%20talents%2C%20and%20even%20flaws.

Seigfried, K. (2013). *The Thor Movies and Norse Mythology.* Norsemyth.org. https://www.norsemyth.org/2013/11/the-thor-movies-and-norse-mythology.html

Sheppard, N. (2009, February 14). *The Origins of the Norse Mythology.* The Norse Gods. https://thenorsegods.com/the-origins-of-the-norse-mythology/

Sheppard, N. (2013, November 20). *Ragnarok.* The Norse Gods. https://thenorsegods.com/ragnarok/

Skald's Keep. (2021a, February 27). *What is Odinism?* Skald's Keep. https://skaldskeep.com/what-is-odinism/

Skald's Keep. (2021b, October 26). *The Norse Runes*. Skald's Keep. https://skaldskeep.com/norse/runes/

Skald's Keep. (2022a, February 12). *Norse Magic*. Skald's Keep. https://skaldskeep.com/norse/magic/#:~:text=Magic%20Magic%20is%20a%20very%20important%20concept%20in,magic%20exist%20in%20Norse%20Paganism%2C%20including%20the%20following%3A

Skald's Keep. (2022b, March 9). *Introduction to Norse Heathenry*. Skald's Keep. https://skaldskeep.com/norse/intro/

Smith, R. (2013). Chapter 1: What Is The Way of Fire & Ice? In *The Way of Fire and Ice*. Google Books. https://books.google.co.za/books?id=u6yrDwAAQBAJ&printsec=frontcover#v=onepage&q&f=false

Smyth, N. (2021, February 19). *Trolldom: The Mystical Healers of Nordic Folklore*. The Unfamiliar Hour. https://unfamiliarhour.wixsite.com/site/post/trolldom-the-mystical-healers-of-nordic-folklore

Snorri Sturluson, Sigurður Nordal, & Young, J. I. (1964). *The prose Edda of Snorri Sturluson : tales from Norse mythology*. Berkeley.

*The Indo-European Family*. (n.d.). Compendium of Language Management in Canada (CLMC). Retrieved April 14, 2022, from https://www.uottawa.ca/clmc/indo-european-family#:~:text=The%20term%20Indo-European%20was%20introduced%20in%201816%20by

The Norwegian American. (2017, November 2). *Viking Symbols "Stolen" by Racists - The Norwegian American*. The Norwegian American. https://www.norwegianamerican.com/viking-symbols-stolen-racists/

*The Viking Age*. (2022). National Museum of Denmark. https://en.natmus.dk/historical-knowledge/denmark/prehistoric-period-until-1050-ad/the-viking-age/

Thursatru. (2014). *What Is Thursatru?* Thursatru. https://www.thursatru.com/whatisthursatru

Time Nomads. (2021, June 20). *Norse Paganism for Beginners: Quick Introduction + Resources*. Time Nomads | Your Pagan Store Online. https://www.timenomads.com/norse-paganism-for-beginners/#norse-pagan-paths

Two Wander. (2020a, April 22). *A Beginner's*

*Guide To Astrology And How To Use It To Bring Balance To Your Life*. Two Wander. https://www.twowander.com/blog/beginners-guide-astrology-bring-balance-to-life

Two Wander. (2020b, July 4). *How To Use Tarot Cards For Stress Management*. Two Wander. https://www.twowander.com/blog/how-to-use-tarot-cards-for-stress-management

Two Wander. (2020c, November 25). *Rune Meanings And How To Use Rune Stones For Divination*. Two Wander. https://www.twowander.com/blog/rune-meanings-how-to-use-runestones-for-divination

Viking Chamber. (2018). *Top 8 Viking Norse Germanic Holidays*. Vikingchamber.org. http://vikingchamber.org/top-8-viking-norse-germanic-holidays

Von See, K. (1998). Snorri Sturluson and the Creation of a Norse Cultural Ideology. In *Jstor.org* (pp. 363–393). https://www.jstor.org/stable/48613195?seq=1

Wigington, P. (2017a). *Learn About the Norse Eddas and Sagas*. Learn Religions. https://www.learnreligions.com/norse-eddas-and-sagas-2561561

Wigington, P. (2017b). *Learn the Basics Behind*

*the Norse Runes*. Learn Religions. https://www.learnreligions.com/norse-runes-basic-overview-2562815

Wigington, P. (2017c). *Norse Deities*. Learn Religions. https://www.learnreligions.com/norse-deities-4590158

Wigington, P. (2017d). *The 9 Noble Virtues of Asatru*. Learn Religions. https://www.learnreligions.com/noble-virtues-of-asatru-2561539

Wigington, P. (2017e). *What is the Asatru Pagan Tradition?* Learn Religions. https://www.learnreligions.com/asatru-modern-paganism-2562545

Wikipedia Contributors. (2021). Æsir–Vanir War. In *Wikipedia*. Wikimedia Foundation. https://en.wikipedia.org/wiki/%C3%86sir%E2%80%93Vanir_War

Wikipedia Contributors. (2022a). Old Norse religion. In *Wikipedia*. Wikimedia Foundation. https://en.wikipedia.org/wiki/Old_Norse_religion

Wikipedia Contributors. (2022b). Edda. In *Wikipedia*. Wikimedia Foundation. https://en.wikipedia.org/wiki/Edda

Wikipedia Contributors. (2022c). Sigyn. In *Wikipedia*. Wikimedia Foundation.

https://en.wikipedia.org/wiki/Sigyn

Wikipedia Contributors. (2022d). Norse rituals. In *Wikipedia*. Wikimedia Foundation. https://en.wikipedia.org/wiki/Norse_rituals

Wikipedia Contributors. (2022e). Ynglinga saga. In *Wikipedia*. Wikimedia Foundation. https://en.wikipedia.org/wiki/Ynglinga_saga

Wikipedia Contributors. (2022f). Heimskringla. In *Wikipedia*. Wikimedia Foundation. https://en.wikipedia.org/wiki/Heimskringla

Witch Path Forward. (2018). *Asatru*. Witch Path Forward. http://www.witchpathforward.com/asatru.html

# OTHER BOOKS BY HISTORY BROUGHT ALIVE

- Ancient Egypt: Discover Fascinating History, Mythology, Gods, Goddesses, Pharaohs, Pyramids, and More from the Mysterious Ancient Egyptian Civilization.

Available now on Kindle, Paperback, Hardcover & Audio in all regions.

- Greek Mythology: Explore The Timeless Tales Of Ancient Greece, The Myths, History & Legends of The Gods, Goddesses, Titans, Heroes, Monsters & More

Available now on Kindle, Paperback, Hardcover & Audio in all regions.

- Mythology for Kids: Explore Timeless Tales, Characters, History, & Legendary Stories from Around the World. Norse, Celtic, Roman, Greek, Egypt & Many More

Available now on Kindle, Paperback, Hardcover & Audio in all regions.

- Mythology of Mesopotamia: Fascinating Insights, Myths, Stories & History From The World's Most Ancient Civilization. Sumerian, Akkadian, Babylonian, Persian, Assyrian and More

Available now on Kindle, Paperback, Hardcover & Audio in all regions.

- Norse Magic & Runes: A Guide To The Magic, Rituals, Spells & Meanings of Norse Magick, Mythology & Reading The Elder Futhark Runes

Available now on Kindle, Paperback, Hardcover & Audio in all regions.

- Norse Mythology, Vikings, Magic & Runes: Stories, Legends & Timeless Tales From Norse & Viking Folklore + A Guide To The Rituals, Spells & Meanings of Norse Magick & The Elder Futhark Runes. (3 books in 1)

Available now on Kindle, Paperback, Hardcover & Audio in all regions.

- Norse Mythology: Captivating Stories & Timeless Tales Of Norse Folklore. The Myths, Sagas & Legends of The Gods, Immortals, Magical Creatures, Vikings &

More

Available now on Kindle, Paperback, Hardcover & Audio in all regions.

- Norse Mythology for Kids: Legendary Stories, Quests & Timeless Tales from Norse Folklore. The Myths, Sagas & Epics of the Gods, Immortals, Magic Creatures, Vikings & More

Available now on Kindle, Paperback, Hardcover & Audio in all regions.

- Roman Empire: Rise & The Fall. Explore The History, Mythology, Legends, Epic Battles & Lives Of The Emperors, Legions, Heroes, Gladiators & More

Available now on Kindle, Paperback, Hardcover & Audio in all regions.

- The Vikings: Who Were The Vikings? Enter The Viking Age & Discover The Facts, Sagas, Norse Mythology, Legends, Battles & More

Available now on Kindle, Paperback, Hardcover & Audio in all regions.

# FREE BONUS BOOK FROM HBA: EBOOK BUNDLE

Greetings!

First of all, thank you for reading our books. As fellow passionate readers of History and Mythology, we aim to create the very best books for our readers.

Now, we invite you to join our VIP list. As a welcome gift, we offer the History & Mythology Ebook Bundle below for free. Plus you can be the first to receive new books and exclusives! Remember it's 100% free to join.

Simply scan the QR code to join.

*NORSE PAGANISM FOR BEGINNERS*

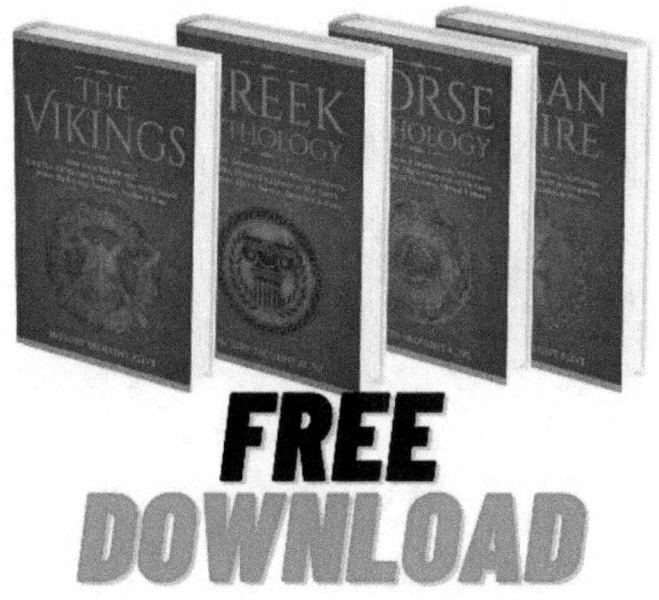

Keep up to date with us on:

YouTube: History Brought Alive

Facebook: History Brought Alive

www.historybroughtalive.com

www.ingramcontent.com/pod-product-compliance
Lightning Source LLC
Chambersburg PA
CBHW071607080526
44588CB00010B/1047